Antlers in Space

and Other Common Phenomena

Antlers in Space

and Other Common Phenomena

Essays by Melissa Wiley

Split Lip Press

Published by Split Lip Press
333 Sinkler Road
Wyncote, PA 19095
www.splitlippress.com

ISBN: 978-1-5426514-7-9

Cover Art by Jayme Cawthern

For Robert

Table of Contents

Fugue

Visions of Animals

Orisons

Fugue

1. a musical composition in which one or two themes are repeated or imitated by successively entering voices and contrapuntally developed in a continuous interweaving of the voice parts

2. a disturbed state of consciousness in which the one affected seems to perform acts in full awareness but upon recovery cannot recollect the acts performed

"Air, I should explain, becomes wind when it is agitated." —*Lucretius*

The Memory of Water

The problem begins and ends with beauty. The row to and from. The walk back to your room from the dock comes later. For now, there is the cradle of the canoe for you to row yourself through a pond in the shape of a kidney bean. Only the woman who paddles herself out is not the same who paddles back. The first gazes only at her face's reflection in the water's sheer tarpaulin; the second looks for turtles among the rocks. She strains her eyes when one shell leaps atop another so there is only one turtle with two heads for a time.

Too quick, too quick for any fun, she thinks with a shake of her head, only the thinnest of wool left blanketing her skull. She bends sideways at the waist, preparing to pour herself like a pitcher, to water the water beneath her. Parting her lips, she hangs her arm over the boat's rim, dangling a finger in the shallows, as she watches the ripples lengthen into ribbon.

Our canoes are all we have in the end, perhaps I should mention. Only once there is an end, there is no more rowing, even if our boats do remain rocking among the sands. Half slunk onto shore, half submerged among kidney bean cytoplasm, these wooden wombs are what we fold ourselves into softly as bath towels while staring at the crevice beneath our knee caps, the slit where a puppeteer would thread his string were we unable to row ourselves back to where we began.

Only this is not yet the end—not yet, not yet—because we are only rowing from one end of the Guggenheim to the other, getting a little paddle happy while making the other patrons wait longer than they wish. Any art worth the price of admission, however, moves through water, which still makes all the world so light, so weightless I can still remember standing on the fringes of an emerald lake holding my mother like a baby in my arms. Why the central exhibit was a herd of taxidermied deer running across the museum's walls don't ask me, not when there was so much water only a floor above them.

My mother's last summer of life was almost at an end, and I decided she would not see New York City before dying as she wanted. I denied her last wish, because she also would have closed her eyes against the strobe lights pulsing from the chandelier of floating cars at Guggenheim's entrance. She also would have thought there was nothing much to see here—only frozen car wrecks and fiberglass-stuffed deer fleeing a hunter always absent— nothing at all apart from the line to the indoor canoe ride, where a woman wearing a dress looking like an apron took longer navigating a Styrofoam island than she needed. My mom too, I am now nearly certain, would have splashed water on her arms the same as I did once she rounded the leer of the exit sign with no intention yet of leaving. Because there is little need to visit any museum unless you get a little wet in the process.

She too would have left the Guggenheim in more than a small hurry to row yet farther, yet faster at the foot of the Loeb Boathouse, where she could drape a leg over the canoe's edge, letting her toe hair uncurl itself beside the turtles on the rocks smelling of fresh turtle soup, because they do nothing all day long there except sit baking like bread in the sun. I can still see her smiling with the yellow archipelago of extra enamel on her right front tooth catching a swift whippoorwill of light, if she only could have hurried.

Only I wanted to row beneath the bridges of Central Park without her hairy toes for resistance. I wanted to avoid her asking me to slow my momentum so she could stare at turtles sunbathing. Not New York, I told her, where I have since rowed with such speed I have seen nothing but olive oviform blurs out the corner of my vision, only jagged hints of a skyline behind them.

When she said she wanted to see the Statue of Liberty, I had been to New York only once for the weekend. Still that was enough for me to know it wasn't the city for terminal cancer patients. Not with my mom wearing her surgical socks and her neck crooked so far forward she couldn't drink Diet Coke from a can, so I always had to carry a straw inside my pocket. If she wanted to go somewhere for her last Labor Day weekend, we were going to Asheville, I said, caring nothing for North Carolina or its rash of pine trees too prickly to touch and wrap your arms around them.

I chose Asheville based on a coworker's recommendation, though I had as little love for this woman in my office as I did for any city without a subway system. Still we were going to Asheville, I decided, because the Biltmore Estate had wheelchair access, because this was where Charlton Heston once resided, though we had watched *The Ten Commandments* one Thanksgiving and agreed once was all we needed. My mother had driven to Asheville with her own mother ten years before this and hadn't thought it worth returning, she softly mentioned.

When I turned five, she paid for swimming lessons so I could splash around the pool three times in succession, and afterward I gave her my own lesson. I taught her to jump inside the lake where my dad caught catfish without pinching her nose, to keep her face below water's surface while swimming to where her toes couldn't touch any clams on lake's bottom. Only she never could manage, even when I told her to pay closer attention. She tried but couldn't, and I settled for holding her a moment, for not letting her drown in water three feet deep, though she only laughed, saying she was too fat for that to happen.

Within two months of her diagnosis, cancer had deflated the wobbly tire encircling her abdomen, making her too thin to float. And everyone knows Manhattan is an island, with swamp creatures encroaching its edges. Safer then to keep her captive, among the hills of North Carolina at the close of an exceptionally dry summer. Better to keep her hemmed by forests, where her canoe's holes wouldn't fill with water and sink us all with her.

Beside a pile of board games in the parlor of our bed and breakfast we read the house was once the home of Charlton Heston. Moses, who lobbied for gun rights once he finished breaking stone tablets, had slept in our bed. Stretching from beneath our mattress to the bathroom's clawfoot tub, one floorboard was singed black with a cigar butt in three places. We read he had made a habit of putting them out on the floor. We read this on another plaque behind a vase of silk flowers with dust for pollen. We were learning so much here, among the desiccation.

The rose gardens of the Biltmore Estate were jaundiced with a fresh leakage of bile the afternoon we visited. We found a beard's coarse bristle where a few weeks prior all was plush and verdant. The flower beds had since been charred to ashes without the expenditure of any active violence. As we sat at the gardens' center, on a bench whose wood had begun to splinter, my mom braided and weakly unbraided her fingers. She pressed her thumbnail into my cuticles, one by one. She reminded me to push them back into sickle moons every night before falling asleep again. Otherwise, they would shrink each evening as my dreams lengthened. My nails, though, have since shrunken so I can scarcely see them. Their tips all have serrated edges, because I bend them back when they grow longer than I like. They are nails too rough and too tiny to bother painting. They look yellow as Asheville grass when I peel an orange and the rind clings to the skin beneath them. I let her push all my cuticles back then, however. I let her attempt to beautify something certain to become an eyesore the moment she looked the other direction. My sweet, short mother with the long, pink nails who cared nothing, I believe, about the grass's yellowing.

Yet however grieved you may be for the dying woman sleeping at our side in a mansion with cigar stains marking the path between the bed and bath, the veins of your wrists still reticulate into smooth, alluvial plains. Unless you yourself are dying, your skin remains smooth as marble to the touch. It remains incapable of wilting in the heat, no matter how hot and dry the summer, how small and square your nails, with no suggestion of sickle moons at their bases.

Your body temperature stays constant while the surrounding vegetation is stained so bleak a lemon that all fruit begins to taste the same, apples and oranges equally void of acid.

Until you start decaying, until you watch the turtles of Central Park copulate with a blistering kind of wonder, your own life still means more than those that are dwindling away. Yet you slow the swinging of your oars a moment to stare into eyes just beginning to look out from beneath their shells. The eyes look sadder because they know their beauty's meaning. They sparkle with awareness you would hardly meet their gaze were something inside you not also dying.

Some scientists posit that water bears the imprint of every person who touches it forever afterward. They claim it retains a living memory of each one of us who performs a half-conscious ablution. Scarred by an influx of intimacy, pockmarked by everything we are ourselves, water is more empathic than any gods in any heavens. However lonely or unloved you may find yourself in a world without your mother, wash your hands in the bathroom sink and you are carried into the very oceans, where you open your eyes beneath the surge of waves above and plug your nose and see her swimming, a mermaid with skin smooth as marble, smoother than yours has ever been. You see her smiling with the innocence of the baby you once held in your arms at lake's membrane. She says nothing to you except that she is waiting to drive with you to Asheville again. Only you have already booked a flight to New York instead. You haven't rowed yourself past the Bethesda Terrace fountain in far too many months on end. You haven't taken hold of the oars in longer than you like to imagine, just to feel the spray of water that remembers when your arms were sturdy as the ribs of a canoe, when you were strong enough to hold a woman three times your weight.

My last afternoon in New York several months ago, I spent sitting beside my best friend, Ella. We were lazing on her couch flipping through the

Kama Sutra. From the kitchen, her husband shouted a couple in Shanghai had fallen into a sea of traffic while having sex against a window. I laughed, saying at least they died in a happy position, then poured myself more coffee. Earlier that morning, we bought two brown paper bags brimming with whole beans from a Puerto Rican shop beneath whose awning I watched a man wheel another male body lying still and sheeted into the basement of the mortuary next door. When the door closed behind them, I stood up from a bench the same length as the gurney and stretched my arms above my head, reminding my muscles to take in more oxygen. I spotted a neon sign across the street advertising Malaysian massages and told Ella I'd meet her in an hour or so back at her apartment.

Stepping through the entrance, walking through a veil of tortoiseshell beads hanging from the ceiling, I faced three leather chairs with buckets of water at their feet. Seeing a honey-haired woman with eyes twitching behind their lids at the chair farthest from the entrance, I sat in the middle. I told the man behind the desk I wanted half an hour's foot massage if he had the time for it.

Hanging on the wall behind him was a chart tracing the connection of every nerve in the body to one corresponding in the feet. The print was too small for me to read without squinting, and I closed my eyes as he kneaded each of my toes in turn. I let the dream floods come, let my eyes twitch with shocks of lightning.

At half hour's end, the masseur swaddled my feet in a hot towel then held them in his arms a moment, waiting for the blood to drain from my toes back toward my thighs. He placed my feet on the stool again, orbited both my knees with a forefinger, and smiled, piping, Friend, now we go pat pat? And I nodded, saying, Yes, I want pat pat. Very much.

He led me down the hall to a room lit into a barren purple planet and said, Friend, gesturing to the bed at room's center, over which lay a white towel thin as a crepe. He had exhausted all his English, though I knew to take off all my clothes except for my panties and leave them on the folding chair in a heap. I knew to lie prone, dissolving from a rock into a lake. I knew too there would be some pain in this. I knew, as the chart promised, my feet's nerve endings connected to every other part of my body and I would have saved myself money by getting only a foot massage instead.

I spent the extra only for his hands to probe the twin crooks of my shoulder blades and the rise of my waist to my buttocks. The room's purple silence, the strange hands stroking my bare topography were New York to me as much as the pond in Central Park, the part I wanted all to myself and without my mother still. When he turned me over, I kept my eyes closed and lips parted for a kiss from the air alone, knowing that even were he to enter me and attempt to fill all my spaces, the emptiness inside me is too deep for any one phallus to fill completely. The body is 60 percent water, my bloodstream a purveyor of memories tinged scarlet.

Later that day, a bruise began spreading across my lower hip where I had twice asked my masseur to press harder. Two hours before the play Ella and I were to see started, I walked stiff with pain inside Chez Josephine, a bistro on west 42nd Street named for Josephine Baker. Born forty years before my mother, Josephine played the eponymous heroine in the movie *Zouzou*, which I have watched on three successive Thanksgivings in lieu of *The Ten Commandments*.

In the movie's most memorable scene, Zouzou warbles a lachrymose aria as she swings inside a steel bird cage, white feathered tassels warming her nipples and gossamer wings sprouting out her back. The cage is just large enough to accommodate her legs as she extends her body nearly supine to linger on a high note better fit for canaries. At song's end, she dives out of the cage onto two sets of outstretched male arms. She opens wide her ribs and bows to the audience. Fully a woman now, a mere winged chansonnier no longer.

The bistro's azure walls were all immured in black and white photographs of Josephine. A cascade of candelabras receded past a piano to the back wall, where we were seated beside a mahogany pig, its insides filleted to accommodate a bouquet of artificial hydrangeas. The first to step inside, I was the first greeted by the maître d', who wore a crimson kimono. Beneath a mirror reflecting piano keys arranged into a too perfect show of teeth no one was playing, he confirmed the reservation. He turned on his slipper heel and led us to our table, where he pulled out my chair with a flourish of his flaccid silk wing.

We ordered a bottle of wine, an appetizer, an entrée to divide between us. Minutes later, a party of eight elderly women padded into our same corner of the room. With their hair tinted blue, their spines hunched into shepherd's crooks over their menus, they looked the natural inhabitants of this intimate homage to the demi monde of long, long ago. After the waiter filled their wine glasses, they toasted to Josephine. They clinked their goblets with arthritic grace and drank with a relish only those who have known life within and without the bird cage can know. The song does not die out inside the body for the wires that encase it. We all also wish to paddle a little longer than the time we're given.

Despite having coiffed their hair into sausage-curl nests, despite wearing their family diamonds, their faces were molting, visibly crumbling into carrion while their gaze stayed steady. They were rowing slowly as limestone turning to marble while looking out onto the slattern rocks. Each searched for her own mother among the turtles of Central Park, and I watched them stretch their necks in the sun, using only their legs for oars.

Milk from a Chicken

In Belize, I ate a plate of fresh papaya cut into oblong cubes each morning while shifting the legs of my chair in the sand. Papaya, I said aloud to waves rubbing the rock. Papaya, the name I would give myself were my skin only a brighter shade of orange, were my navel only overgrown with a fistula of black seeds begun to swarm.

As it was, I reminded our waiter, Tua, of my real name each morning, because he kept forgetting then asking me again. Melissa, though, is Greek for honeybee, and the bee that alchemizes milkweed nectar into honey dies the moment you step barefoot on its thorax in the grass. And that is something worth remembering, the price that must be paid for sweetness.

Papaya, however, needs no honey, and Belizean bread tastes better without jam, butter only. So I repeated my name and asked Tua for milk with my coffee. Chicken milk, he added, laughing through his Buddha belly. And I laughed back from the flapping lid of my larynx, wondering what chicken breasts were good for besides a fatter piece of meat.

For a week, my husband and I slept in a cabana at a yoga resort where we practiced no yoga yet stretched our arms out to the seagrass soon after waking. Done with breakfast and leaving Tua until next morning, I asked the manager for a safety pin so my dress would cover more of my skin dividing one half of my cherry-print dress from the other with too much whiteness. Only the pin left a womb-shaped gap between the cotton. Some flesh hung helpless among cherries suspended in ink. Left to itself, ripe fruit too is a wild thing, hanging inert on the vine for only so long a time. To pick cherries is also to invite worms into your pie. I know because I've done so myself hundreds of times.

Later in the day, after hours of swimming, we rode bikes we'd rented toward San Pedro for dinner at dusk. My handlebars were rusted, my brakes' legs receded into stumps, and I sped over the road's rock clumps as if they were grass hummocks.

After eating, we watched men place bets on which one of nine squares a chicken would shit when nervous. We remounted our bikes and circled women in braids selling lavalieres of lizards carved from the shells of conches, shaking our heads no, no thank you, while secretly wanting to cradle such lizards polished pink to blushing, to hang them from our necks close to where our pulse kept our bodies' rhythm.

As we passed the glow of the hardware store on the edge of town at nine in the evening, the world became lightless. We confronted a stretch of blackness as our ears fizzed with insects. Three hours earlier on this same roadway, we'd sung and held a high, clear note that echoed off the derelict buildings. We'd done this while riding over the rocks simply to hear our voices ululate without making the effort of any real wailing. Crepuscular rays pink as bleeding gums, though, force you to sing. Darkness begs for the cold quiver of silence.

We pedaled through the blackness in a hush. Only as the road became a receding wall we felt sure we might collide with, my husband shouted at me to slow down. Better to walk, he said, considering our new blindness. Better yet to ride back to the hardware store, which against all odds still was open. Better to buy a flashlight and walk the three miles remaining.

Instead of listening, I pressed my warmth against my handlebars and rode the faster on. Without any light to see each other, better I pedal with enough speed so he wouldn't crash into me and we tumble down together. Though of this there was little danger, me with the stronger if shorter legs. Me with my body closer to the ground, the less far to topple.

The road too was straight if furrowed. A string of scalloped lights overhanging a restaurant a mile and a half in the distance serving only lionfish, an invasive predator covered in quills like a hedgehog grown gills for

16

amphibiousness, would alert us we were halfway back to our cabana. The lights were dim yet orange as a sunset to lure in diners, because where the light is next to nothing, odds are there is a woman lowering her eyes at a man she imagines touching her where she is softest. And we would see the lights if not the woman beneath them, a woman wearing a dress printed with fruit leaching its own juices.

As a young girl in my innocence, I once plucked cherries from a tree I could see from my bedroom window, cherries so red they looked swollen with magma to me. Late afternoons, I stood on a wooden ladder with rungs spaced wide as hippo teeth. Dropping a jumble of cherries into a tin bucket, I ate half or more of them while standing, so the pies were often slimmer than my mom liked. I bit through any number of worms wriggling their way to a pit, hoping I had swallowed the worm half that would not regrow inside my stomach. They regenerated the same as starfish arms, I'd read while wanting to forget it. Each worm could grow a new head but not replace its sexual organs. Its life was all too easily extended only to lose all desire for it.

Worms or no worms swimming through your intestines, cherry pie is a blessed thing to eat early of a morning. And too many summers ago to feel quite real at present, I ate two or three slices for breakfast while overlooking the steel glint of silos and white barn beyond them. Each cherry rested so round and whole on my tongue, it is little wonder I have since bought so many cherry-print dresses. At least, I tell myself, I have a reason.

All the cherry trees, though, have long since fallen. First the one outside my bedroom was rent by lightning, a tree I had long thought of as a person, dead and gone before I turned eleven. Then both my parents were flattened by diseases. The farm we lived on fell down with them.

I still hunger for the cherry pie I no longer eat for breakfast while drinking coffee. Now I'm less a believer of dressing my age than of dressing my favorite fruit, which I no longer pick fresh from a tree plagued with worms in place of the serpents of Eden. And I may be ripe now past plucking, but of all the world's colors, cherry red is the last to fade into nothing, into a road so lightless and bumpy it was a wonder I didn't blow a tire that Belizean evening. I also had my safety pin, so I looked less like bursting than before I drank the milk of a chicken.

After riding back somehow safely to our cabana then falling asleep, next day we walked to a burger bar where $10 bought a bucket of beer and an hour's drinking inside an inner tube the color of papaya begun rotting. Most women ordered in bikinis while I wore the same dress as the day before. My safety pin had come undone, though, my husband whispered gently.

The woman with the smallest bikini and seeming the drunkest shouted that today was her birthday. She called for a free round of cherry vodka shots from a bartender whose smile seemed to say he didn't believe her but wouldn't argue with someone so pretty. She eyed my dress and insisted I drink with her, when I wished her many happy returns while secretly hoping we would no longer have to keep speaking.

A few days later, we stopped our bikes for bottled water at a beachfront tavern. Seeing me stare at a silver snake curled inside a clear bottle of liquor, the bartender offered me a taste. The snake was imported from Vietnam and dead before I was likely born, he told me. If I had a sore throat, a viper shot would cure it in the way of all good poison. Even if my throat felt fine, I'd find myself smiling. I laughed and said no thank you, though for a moment I was tempted. Because I was again wearing the cherry dress and a viper looks a small serpent. Because a cherry is only an apple shrunken into a sweetness I eat no more for breakfast. Because there is an ache that comes with absence.

Showering outdoors beneath a mango tree our last morning, I watched two iguanas mate on the soap dish beside me. The male mounted a female looking his mirror image. He stepped on her tail to keep himself inside her until he was done thrusting, until runnels of semen from a reptile ignoring a woman beside him, naked and laughing, filtered down the drain with my shampoo. I laughed because my throat had begun hurting and my only cure was poison.

Later, I ate my last plate of papaya, which Tua served then asked again if I wanted chicken milk with my coffee. That afternoon, we would bike once more to San Pedro, past the bar selling liquor infused with a viper, with my throat sore and aching. Again, I would not drink the venom offered.

Courtesans in New Orleans

All my life I'll know I ignored them, my cousin Kevin and his wife on Royal Street in New Orleans. Nothing could have been simpler than saying hello to them. Instead, I turned toward Jackson Square and away from all the street musicians.

Kevin's beard had gone gray in patches. Gibbous moons bleached tired jowls hung heavy as damask curtains. He looked as if he'd gained thirty pounds since last time I'd seen him. I used to wonder how he found Courtney attractive. The hair on her head curled the same as that on my labia while her calves closed over feet without ankles to interrupt them. Now they looked so similar, their bodies equally shapeless, I imagined real sympathy thickened between them. They stood drinking beer from plastic cups, their lower lips both hung slack as those of groupers changing sexes.

Once a female grouper grows to eight inches, she becomes a male lusting on his former female companions. Kevin and Courtney made love like sleeping fish, I supposed, with their eyes always open. They closed them for hours afterward to replenish moisture when breathing through their noses.

As they wrapped arms around each other's waists blurred into their buttocks, I sucked air from my stomach deeper inside a dress I'd bought near where Courtney and Kevin were standing when I saw them, each with their legs spread wide to prevent them rolling my direction. My dress was tight and olive, yet from the back Kevin would never recognize his cousin. Ten years after my father's funeral and he knew next to nothing of me or others not as happy and corpulent.

In our hotel, my husband and I slept better in the day than at night after we'd both had too much to drink without waking dehydrated. After dusk, our bodies' heat also grew more visible to bugs that ravaged us only in darkness. Maybe they were lice, maybe bedbugs, though if so we were the ones who brought them. We were their hosts, with no way of leaving our skins, not even in New Orleans.

They'd attacked us the past three weeks in our Chicago apartment, where my husband kept telling me to make it a meditation. He did this because my bites swelled while his stayed too small to notice and he didn't want to pay for fumigation. Yet sleep was becoming less and less of a respite, to the point I couldn't help but wonder what would happen once my eyelids atrophied into a gossamer hymen. Time and again, I asked myself how I'd survive once I was forced to sleep with my eyes always open. I asked myself without answering the question, because I am not a fish but remain a woman.

We bought bug spray to combat every possible pestilence, spraying until we choked on fumes we read might be cancerous. Cancer, though, we were fine with so long as it allowed us to sleep while our eyelids were still with us. The insects we would rather be phantasms, something one article suggested—a sign of psychosis—only slowed their hunger to a grazing once we emptied two bottles within minutes. We were depleting the supplies of all the Walgreens within a five-mile radius.

It's been a month now since we've returned from New Orleans. I still feel them crawling down every orifice, which could also signal the beginning of multiple sclerosis, I've gleaned from sundry sources. Whatever my verdict, even that they'll leave us once we move all our furniture into another apartment, the body's reality remains primary, the feeling of teeth marks along your wrists the same as being bitten.

Rain was predicted for all three days of our trip to New Orleans. At least there, though, we could escape some of the stinging, from the bugs themselves or our nerves begun to blink like electrical wire frayed by rodents. In Chicago, I'd begun seeing blue sparks rioting along our blanket. Maybe they were small bug bodies glowing as they fed on my thighs and stomach, maybe only the exchange of static electricity. Or maybe every small movement now hurts me. I wake with twice as many bites as my husband if we go a night without spraying.

Some things, though, had to be simpler in the Big Easy, where the wind is warmer so close to the Mississippi River. On our flight from O'Hare to Louis Armstrong on Christmas morning, I sat between two older men while my husband sat two rows behind me. The man on my left resembled a long-dead great uncle and worked a crossword puzzle. The other played solitaire, shuffling the cards with his finger across his phone screen. I put my head down on the tray table, tired of wanting more love than was given, tired of hoping for love to multiply into an insect colony embedded deep within my mattress no amount of poison would poison completely.

As we were dressing for dinner later that evening, our first in New Orleans since a couple years before, I told my husband I thought my sister, whom we had recently visited, had become so radiant I had to squint when I saw her lately. He smiled, nodding his agreement. She was a beautiful woman, he added, though looked nothing like me.

I was applying mascara in the bathroom when I wondered if my husband realized my eyes were not brown but golden while ringed in aquamarine, like a cow paddy eclipsing the ocean. Only I didn't bother asking, because my sister's are rounder and yet more golden and see better too while mine both have astigmatisms. At dinner, however, he reraised the subject, saying my sister had such a pretty face and he didn't understand how people assumed we were related. I ate my gumbo and kept silent. I had tried applying my mascara carefully, but a streak had settled in a crack below my eye, I later noticed. There's no real help, though, for a face molded this crudely. I'm the oldest sister, the oldest of all the cousins.

The courtesans of Venice, I read once in a magazine, walked the city's crowded streets on stilts when their line of customers grew low. Three heads taller than other pedestrians, they knew if they fell it would only be into the arms of a stranger who would likely pay their next month's rent and grocery bill also. Famously erudite and speaking many languages, they walked certain they need not do so long among so many faces upturned to watch a woman too alluring to be too virtuous.

Yet stand close enough to another person's face and her pores become the more obvious, the endless holes through which her skin breathes. You see all too clearly the loveliest woman in the room is only a series of spaces through which you may fall or keep your balance, courtesans no more solid a body than anyone less amorous.

And as I sat there, chewing softened rice with sausage, I told myself I was wrong to have come to a place where life is meant to be less difficult because there is so much music. I realized I bought airplane tickets only to travel somewhere I looked less porous to strangers who saw me only at a distance. I traveled the same as a soul who kept self-killing, who reincarnated in yet more broken bodies only to commit the selfsame carnage. Wherever I went now too, bugs on my skin came with me.

Kevin and Courtney, my sister later told me, had a young daughter I didn't see while I saw them watching a woman play ukulele. Maybe her grandparents were babysitting her in Indianapolis, where they'd bought a house, my sister also told me. I was glad in any case not to have to meet her and pretend she was pretty. Whatever she looked like as a toddler or baby, she stood little chance of attracting men better looking than her father once she entered adolescence. The odds she'd become a man when she grew taller were higher than average.

I told myself this was the last year I could visit New Orleans and wear something slutty, if only because I'm three years older than Courtney. Buying dresses, though, almost too small for me is what I do when my skin itches, when I feel myself unraveling. They allow me to enjoy for a little longer this body, whose eyelids I blink only to ensure they haven't started thinning prematurely.

When I slipped into the dress I bought the evening before I saw Kevin and Courtney, my husband said it fit me tightly as a Band-Aid. The color too resembled military camouflaging, and I hardly needed to spend the money. Wasn't there something better I could be doing? Didn't I need to start saving? Didn't I need bandaging? I asked without listening for any response he made.

After I bought the dress, I stood outside the shop and watched a block of dry ice dissolve down a sewer drain. Gray plumes clouded an oyster bar ringed with a wrought-iron balcony. Dry ice passes from solid to gas directly, refusing to liquefy in a watery purgatory. It sublimates itself into vapor, and I have long been seeking the same, the same metamorphosis into purity, but have given up trying. I've abandoned living for the soul rather than the body, done with extracting meaning from pain. I've stopped trying to be better person than one who runs to New Orleans to buy another dress she doesn't need. A drab Army green.

When I was seven or eight, my vagina began to burn and itch one evening, interrupting my sleep then worsening through the ensuing weeks. I never knew why—a yeast infection probably, from a wet swimsuit worn for too many successive days so it never finished drying—but I lived wordlessly with the burning, unaware of vaginal creams, unaware still partially what it was that was itching. Only when I rode my bicycle down the gravel roads radiating from our farmhouse like phosphenes did the bicycle seat light another fire I had no way of cooling. Wild dogs chased me, snapping at my ankles rotating faster with my bicycle chain.

Two Dobermans overtook me while one nipped at my leg. I rode into a ditch, deciding to let them have their way with me. I rode into a ditch so I wouldn't have to keep living with the fear of them attacking me every time I left my driveway. Once they ate me, they would also end the burning

24

between my legs. I crashed headlong into the sharp grasses, vowing to remain there until the dogs had bloodied all their teeth with me.

When they didn't follow me but left me there crying, I didn't have the courage to ride back past them. Toward dark, my mom drove and found me. She was too late, however, by several hours. I had already reconciled myself to a death there alone and hungry, because prey can grow just as famished as their predator species. By that time, the dogs had also become friends to me. I had given them all my bones, all my meat.

The wish for a quick end to torment has never left me. Now if my vagina begins burning, I buy myself a tube of cream. Secretly, though, I still want the dogs to come finish me. Rather than keep walking on stilts beginning to wobble, I want to fall into a crowd of men waiting to ravish me.

After dinner at the Pelican Club, where we sat along a gleaming leather banquette beside a piano on whose bench were set pink poinsettias in place of any music, we walked inside the studio of an artist named Adrian, certain he'd forgotten us from our visit two years before. He hugged us both, saying he never forgot a face as we reminded him of our names. A toy train was circling the room carrying a bottle of vodka, and he offered us shots to celebrate our return to the city.

As the liquor ran through me, I looked up at a portrait of Robin Williams, his lineaments drawn in steel with knives, Adrian mentioned. Then I turned toward a picture of Hillary Clinton, looking wistful as if politics were a form of poetry, when Adrian said he only ever drew any person's soul, which was always filled with beauty. He said this implying he painted all his subjects fresh from waking, when their eyes were moistest. Yet his rendering of Robin Williams struck me as sinister looking. He appeared as if he were already planning his hanging, as if his laughter were a cardboard box hiding a kitten with no holes punched through for oxygen. As if he had thrown himself to the dogs years before the public became aware of any suicidal tendencies.

As we left, I looked for Kevin and Courtney and relaxed only when I didn't see anyone of their shape walking our same pathway. I didn't want them to have any of Adrian's vodka after me. I didn't want Courtney to compliment my dress of green gauze that kept me from bleeding.

At Café Amelie late next morning, I noticed my husband's hair was turning grayer in sunlight filtering through waxen leaves that never browned but died fully green. After our waiter asked me twice if I'd like more coffee, my husband pointed to his back as he left us, saying that he would sleep with me. This was in response to an earlier complaint I made that we had hardly any sex since the bugs came. I said nothing about the waiter, only wondered how long before my hair turned as silver as my husband's was now beginning.

The last time I saw Kevin, one of his eyes kept twitching as I told some anecdote about my dad at his wake. I thought the story was funny, while he stood shifting his weight. His eyes were always too close together, closer than necessary. Now one blinked as if he were trying to keep debris from falling down his pupil, that or trying to keep it from drying after fucking Courtney. I started laughing at the end of my story as he drifted toward my sister. I stared at his ear and the pale, hard flower it made.

Any ear folds in on itself like petals around a pistil but takes longer than a violet to wilt and decay. In the absence of flowers then, in too long of too cold months on end, those starved for beauty can be excused for paying more attention to the human ear than they might have done were the wind only warmer. Van Gogh cut his ear off deep in a December frost, when the only blossoms left were those he'd painted the previous summer. And I cannot think this insane, the hunger for the loveliness that has gone missing. Of making a hole in your head while pulling the only surviving flower.

A painter with his watercolors hung from a fence had eyes so blue that when I looked at him I felt as if I were swimming then drowning. My husband was with me—we'd taken another nap together, longer each afternoon—and he fired a fusillade of questions at him regarding his technique. The artist and I kept looking at each other as he answered, and I decided that I loved him. Because his eyes were blue, though I would not have minded were they green. Because they were equally vulnerable to desiccation once his eyelids thinned into nothing. Because he was a little old, though his skin was smooth.

He washed all his watercolors in the bath, he said to my husband. He did this so the colors were running off their pages, so they looked as if they had tried to sublimate themselves into vapors but had become only more liquid. He liked the look of paintings that were water-damaged, he acknowledged, when my husband pressed him for a reason. Me too, I said, in order to look in his eyes again and feel myself afloat in them.

While the calliope started playing, we walked to the riverbed, where no one was sleeping, though I felt tempted.

The Mississippi had grayed since we last visited while becoming more restive. People wearing plastic gloves the color of seaweed were collecting garbage. The seagulls sat stationary in the shallows as the waves around them splashed in ludic spirals, and I wondered why the birds didn't fly with the wind, letting it carry them somewhere with less detritus than in New Orleans. Yet they remained strung along the ripples, song notes left on a page of music, indifferent to whether anyone was playing them.

I could not play the music they had written, only watch it lie silent. Staring into wind, my eyes usually burn and I have to shut them. But the wind here was warmer than we had expected. In warm winds, I can stare longer without blinking. I had almost forgotten.

I saw a man pulling the strings of a puppet struggling to fly a kite no larger than my fist, a kite caught in a hackle of juniper bushes. The puppet's hair was threaded with silver, and the wooden hand holding the kite string twitched with exhaustion. Why the man controlling him didn't release his kite from the twigs I could not fathom.

At first, I thought the puppet wore a small mask. Bending closer, though, I saw that beneath his eyes darker rings only shadowed them, as if he had not slept for longer than I liked to imagine. He was so tired from staring into a kite that kept wrapping itself more tightly around branches forked like lightning that the puppet might well be worried they were about to strike him.

Yet even were the wind cooler, he couldn't blink and restore his vision. His eyelids were carved three-quarter open, well on their way to full recession. He had no choice except to watch women for whom he once had lusted become men before him. With no possibility of real sleep ahead, he had to keep flying a kite being torn by brush, pretending the kite was flying while seeing it disintegrate into paper streams.

Cave Dwellings

One cave dwelling resembles another too closely to bother with very many. This, though, was the same as yesterday. Only our guide was different, younger with shorter sideburns and longer legs. Still my husband disappeared into the vast sandstone cellar with the rest while I stayed above ground drinking hot tea from a cold plastic bottle.

I did not want any more souvenirs, did not want especially a small ceramic statue of tapered fairy chimneys with "Cappadocia" inscribed at its base, as we saw everywhere. On our hike two days before, our guide had asked us again and again what shapes we saw among the towering basalt. All the right answers were animals, most native to Africa and the Amazon, yet they were lingams all, a fact as plain as desire itself.

That morning at breakfast with my husband still asleep, my waiter had pressed such a small statue between two paper napkins and set it leaning against my coffee cup. He whispered it was a present, that he hoped I would visit Turkey again soon. A man wearing a baseball cap at the table beside me looked up from his laptop as I stood to leave without placing my knife and fork parallel as snow skis on my plate. I had my secret from the world now, twin lingams folded inside paper napkins I held at my hip with the mole at its sulcus. I could leave my cutlery in a tangle.

As rain began falling above the underground city, I strayed toward a shop selling fabric dolls without any noses stitched onto their faces. Inside, the shop smelled of aniseed and cardamom, and I picked up the doll I thought looked the loneliest with the most room for a nose should I find one of these here too. I was combing through her hair with my fingers when a woman with a mustard scarf enshrouding a face wizened into a walnut gestured for me to sit beside her on a canvas chair.

Trying to concentrate on the rain and evade her stare, I held the doll more closely as she leaned toward me. Had she only found some beauty, I felt she would not have looked with such raw curiosity, would not have rotated her index finger in a loose orbit at my ear until she pressed on the mole at my right cheek. She pressed as if it were a button that would open a trap door to another woman beneath.

She returned her finger to her lap and began speaking in a high voice from the bottom of her throat. I understood nothing of Turkish yet saw she had only a few bottom teeth, that her tongue swam across her gums like neap tides against sand. I laughed, knowing she would not understand even this in response. I laughed because she had discovered who I was without us being able to speak. She had pushed the mole on my right cheek with force enough to penetrate to the mole on my right hip to match it.

When I was five years old, I decided that when I grew old enough to forget who I was, these moles would remind me. They would be enough. I would put a finger to my cheek, slide my panties off over my right hip, and know I was myself still and no one else. Wherever I was, I would be home then, inside this body.

That I would eventually forget myself was beyond question. What might happen to me was also irrelevant, as it still largely is. Yet palpating one of either two birthmarks with my forefinger, I could feel the light of the sun within the darkest cave, the depth of myself born nameless. There was, I told myself standing naked before my bedroom mirror, nothing so very important to see. Better to live by feel altogether.

I couldn't tell the woman this, however, that I had remembered something so sacred in this rain. Her hand rose from her knees and again her finger pressed into my mole, this time harder. Her fingernail pierced my skin, when I stood and thanked her then hurried across the street to a shop selling rugs and gramophones whose copper horns had oxidized into an emerald patina. A man counting coins behind the counter looked up and fixed his eyes on my breasts, and I knew he would miss the mole on my right hip even if I stood there naked. Unlike the old woman, he had no idea who I was and always had been.

Plants with any sense about them grow toward the sun. They abjure the cold beauty of erect posture for phototropism's lean disfigurement, allowing their spines to become gnarled in the lust for light. Yet if plants grow toward the sun, human bodies grow toward each other. Desire, that is all this growing is. It is why there are fairy chimneys in Cappadocia that are no chimneys at all. It is why people abandoned their underground cities long ago, why there's little need to visit them any longer.

In Rome twelve years earlier, I walked the catacombs behind my professor, a graduate student of theology named Angelo with a pregnant wife he'd left in Chicago for the summer. He came here, he said, to visit a certain seaside town an hour's drive east of Naples where his grandfather had shined shoes and stolen sardines from unmanned dinghies. He himself, however, hailed from so near O'Hare's airstrips that he feared the planes' noses would shatter his bedroom window when he was a boy.

A few hours before our fieldtrip below ground began, I was reading *Middlemarch* on a bath towel in the grass when Angelo's shadow eclipsed the sun lighting my page. As he asked how I could read that for pleasure, I watched his eyes graze my thighs then follow a group of girls into the dining hall. A tabby cat skirted my ankles before leaping onto the fountain's edge beside me where a cherub stood holding a dolphin. Looking down at my book again, I saw the shadow had lifted. Underground, Angelo lingered over crypts no more than four feet long, the graves of children. He said we were looking at our own resting places then waited for his voice to echo through the silence. In no hurry to leave this crypt for daylight whose heat pressed its fingers deep into my shoulders, I listened longer than I need have done for an echo that never sounded.

Next weekend, almost everyone in the dorm had left, as if Rome were, like some small town in the Dakotas, a place to escape as soon as you had the option, as if the catacombs lay too close. Saturday morning with the bathroom to myself, I let the shower curtain hang open to this alluvion of hot indoor rain. I washed my hair in sudsy languor, extending my elbows wide as bows poised to release their arrows while straddling two rusting drains.

The night before, I had taken the bus to the Piazza Navona, where I sat on a plinth rounded by time of its edges and watched tourists have their portraits drawn on thin brown paper. Angelo had knocked at my door while I was gone. He left a note inside the room I shared with a Korean exchange student who had gone to Munich Friday morning and wrote offering to cook me dinner on Saturday, naming seven as the hour. When I knocked on his door, he handed me a glass of cold white wine smelling of lemons.

I no longer remember what he prepared as the main course inside his kitchen with the broken verdigris shutters. I only know I was grateful for its splendor, for the fact that it swam in the aromatic juices of volcanic tomatoes and exhaled warm, vaporous bodies of steam.

Throughout dinner, I asked about his wife and family. Over my second glass of wine, I confided my boyfriend had told me he wasn't falling in love with me in response to a question I have since forgotten. I said that I had looked into his flat, lightless gaze and still sucked on his penis. Angelo asked if I had slept with him, when I said yes, hundreds of times, and he threw up his hands and said I was finished. I asked him why while knocking my wine glass onto the floor by accident. Because you're from Indiana, he faux drawled, sweeping up the broken glass. Girls from Indiana can't sleep with men and not love them. Then he told me the dustpan was in the closet.

After emptying the glass into the waste basket, I stood up and walked over to his nightstand. I studied a picture of his wife in her wedding gown, he in his tuxedo, both foreshortened against the cathedral's domed ceiling, both sets of feet rooted to carpet the color of scar tissue. She's lovely, I effused. He smiled to himself and turned the photograph to the wall. He began kissing my hand, each finger in turn to the nail's pale half moons. Before his lips met the mole on my cheek, I had left the room.

Eight years later, I returned to Rome, leaving my husband alone in our garden apartment with black rats patrolling its threshold. For a week, I stayed at a pensione in the purlieus of the Piazza Navona, a house of ten rooms bordered by long-fingered ferns and owned by an Australian couple who sold Italian textiles to the Sydney elite.

Squeezed beside smooth-faced European couples whispering through raised napkins at breakfast, I sipped my coffee quickly, not allowing it time to cool or be refilled. I had returned to Rome, I told myself, to steep all my body's cells in small Italian pleasures, cats on windowsills and unpasteurized cheeses, while on indefinite furlough. I ate my roll without butter, however. I scurried from the sky-lit room before I had finished chewing it through.

Each day after revisiting the Fontana di Trevi, the Keats and Shelley House, the Sistine Chapel, and finally the catacombs, I lapsed into overlong conversations with the hotel's manager, an Egyptian who had immigrated to Rome as many years ago as I first ventured underground after reading George Eliot in the grass. One evening I walked upstairs around 11 o'clock, when his face registered concern. He asked if I was okay, and I understood the foyer had cameras. He had seen the man who had invited me to dinner on the steps of the Pantheon, whose invitation I had foolishly accepted, pin my arms against a wall before I could wriggle free.

Looking into the hotel manager's wide midnight eyes, however, I found myself wishing he would do the same. I told him I was fine and walked down the marbled corridor to my room and didn't leave for the next two days. I ate nothing except the rolls he set outside my door, rolls I overspread with melted butter using my finger because he had forgotten to leave a knife. I made of the pensione a cave, keeping my windows and curtains closed. I sealed in the sun and felt myself burn without light, growing toward no one.

Early May in Cappadocia, however, is far from hot. The mild air cools once the rain comes. There is no need to venture underground to escape the sun. When I tired of listening to the static of gramophones and the clouds thinned, I walked farther on, to a playground behind the mosque near the entrance to the underground city. I sat kicking my legs beneath a yellow swing, slick from the rain, and shivered. Putting a finger to the mole on my cheek, I began trying to remember who I was.

April's Autumn

Left to themselves, animals shirk the burial ritual. Yet their corpses still stink and must be done away with. When one of our sheep stopped breathing, my dad drove to the corner of a soybean field that straddled a creek that became a river where the land grew happier and hillier in a direction we rarely traveled. Unlocking the door to his truck bed, he stood on its bumper, curling and uncurling his fists, before rolling the body to its edge where the sheep's legs hung low and limp.

He wrapped his arms around the body before dropping it beneath a canopy of maple branches. He dug his hands deep inside his pockets, feeling for a piece of string to wrap around his fingers until they whitened. The string found and then let go of, we scattered brush over the slackened jaw. We carried no shovel and we dug no dirt. Once we had gone, the wild dogs would come.

Although this must have been an almost predictable process, I remember putting a sheep to rest with him no more than two or three times. Nor do I recollect the births of as many animals as I ought, abundantly supplied as our farm was with livestock. Clearer are my memories of stumbling across an afterbirth in spring, an afterbirth streaked with what looked like red seaweed and staining my pant knees. My shoes left stains across the barn lot, where our sheep traced our silos' shadows. They had nothing better to do, from experience I knew.

Jesus is a lamb, any Bible will tell you. He is a lamb but not a sheep, because Jesus never budded horns to bash into another ram for fucking rights to the nearest ewe. His voice stayed high as he mewled among catalpa trees and leapt over cockerels rusting atop their weather vanes. Jesus was always a little too lamblike even for lambs themselves, who all bring money for their wool come a year or two.

In New Zealand, you see more sheep than people, the guidebooks all tell you, which was as good a reason to go there as any. People you find easily enough in the place you're leaving. The summer I left for college, my dad tucked a $100 bill in a King James Bible bound in leather. He told me all the answers were in there if I needed. Ten years later, I took the $100 and exchanged it for a bathing suit with a red bow tied between its breast cups. The Bible I left beside the unwanted paperbacks in my building's laundry room.

A glowing blue pupa at night, our Queenstown pool was flush with children hurtling themselves from the diving board and splashing their parents. There were too many children to swim while hardly swimming. So my husband and I folded ourselves onto our lobby's umber couches and drank red wine after we had finished riding the funicular to mountain's top and steering a luge to its bottom.

In New Zealand's April autumn, even lambs' voices have grown deep enough for their bellows to wake you in the morning. Even young males' horns have sprouted into stunted shafts of light. Were their horns not quite so short and their wool not quite so white, I would have thought them ready to fall into breathlessness beneath their own maple branches, as full-grown creatures always might.

With sheep come sheep dogs for good reason, to guard them from the more savage of their species. Only we never trained our dogs to herd our flock. Instead, we gave them lavender-scented baths in our back porch sink. We raised our sponges and baptized them as best we could for no real reason. And as our dogs were crushed by tractors or stolen, our sheep too began their disappearance.

Wild dogs attacked our flock at night, bounding over the arroyo that became a river hundreds of miles in the distance. They slipped beneath the barn door where our sheep slept on hay softening the concrete. The new dogs we bought to replace the old became half wild themselves then, even as we bathed them. At home my first spring break from college, I watched as our spaniel cleaved a leg off a lamb standing there suckling while I worked a crossword puzzle in our kitchen. I ran outside and beat the dog with a stick. His mouth dripped with blood that mixed with milk still falling from the ewe. Red and white ran together on the gravel like strawberries and cream. Food for only feral things.

The lamb's leg hung from its body by two unraveling sinews as I carried her into our yard and asked my dad to help me. I asked because you cannot bury a living thing, not one with a tongue as pink as this. And though I was as grown then as I thought that I would get, I cried as he told me to go back inside the kitchen. Later I washed the dog in the sink again, plunging my arms in bath water made rosy with the lamb's remnants. I pulled his ears back against his head, watching soap filter down to the drum.

When I was four or five years old, my dad tossed my Raggedy Ann doll above our mantle for what reason I now forget, for what was likely nothing. She fell flat against the clock that rang out the hours of our lives so long as we remembered to wind it. And as my mom placed the doll back gently in my lap, I smoothed her apron and noticed one of her eyes was loosened. My mom promised she would sew it, but this never happened, and I began to love winding my fingers behind the eye held only by a few strings yet seeing farther than the other one, I imagined. Holding Raggedy Ann from behind the retina that came undone, I could also see farther in the distance. Helping to untie my doll's sense of sight, I could feel the sweetness of nearly cutting off my finger's tip by pulling tightly on a strand of something soft.

More remarkable than the sheep outnumbering New Zealand's people are the glow worms outnumbering the sheep. Yet glow worms are no worms at all, only larvae yet to become fireflies living below ground. They cling fast to rock smoothed by rivers running to no ocean. Were you to see them in the daylight, you would not see them. They luminesce from organs otherwise invisible except in a place so lightless. They luminesce only to lure another body near, to meld into a single sapphire flame convulsing against stone.

Sitting on a cool bench inside a boat being drawn deeper into darkness, I looked on at endless elfin holocausts. Bright as infant stars, they returned to me as if I had lost them, though I had never been to New Zealand before. Yet you can know someone without knowing how you know him. You can recognize a glow worm without having seen a glow worm in person. All I know for certain is that I sat feeling rescued from skies blue beyond bearing. I preferred the larval light of worms that are no worms to speak of to the sun for the time being.

Our sheep's eyes glowed green in our headlights' glare. Headlights staring back at headlights, they dimmed into blackness the moment we turned off our truck's ignition. They were black as buttons too by morning, plastic discs I might sew with string and loosen with my finger. And trying to catch fireflies overspreading a bed of tulips, I once found myself facing a sheep darting bolts of green light that seemed to tell me to leave the little luminous bugs alone altogether. Her headlight eyes caught in no headlights of their own.

You hear of nothing but death in New Zealand, you should know before you travel half a world away to get there. You hear of the death of flightless birds over and over, the kiwi and takahe and penguins scaling the rocks of Milford Sound, where we kayaked at night once we grew tired of steering ourselves downhill in a toboggan. Species of fat, splay-toed birds keep going extinct due to predators introduced from the British Isles as part of colonization. For all the sheep you see too, there are that many deaths to come. Because being a common animal doesn't make your life an endless one. Even birds that fly will someday fall forever to the ground. Starlings and sparrows as well as takahe that have spent the whole day clambering up a cairn of tin cans only to survey the wreckage below them.

At my dad's wake, the man who now farms his land told me my dad was not a common man. He didn't offer and I didn't ask for explication,because I knew what he meant to say but couldn't. He meant my dad felt for string in his pockets after he had buried a sheep, whereas the more common among us remain part sheep ourselves, staring at headlights in the driveway and never toward the darkness. We wait for the vultures to come and leave animals to bury themselves.

The eyes of those of us unwilling to starve our fingers of oxygen glow a sour shade of green before turning lightless as buttons come daybreak. My dad's eyes were buttons too come noon. Only they were glass buttons through which light shone through. A blue ring divided his pupil from an ocher iris, a blazing blue I had not seen the like of since visiting the glow worm cave, as near to the bottom of the world as I shall ever likely come. A cave with no worms to speak of. A cave throbbing with the light of two bodies wanting to become one, dripping with larvae sticky to the touch. A cave so far below the luge tracks you would never know it existed if not for the brochures in the hotel lobby. Such concentration of love often being buried beyond finding.

Newborn lambs bleat while they spring high into the April air blanketing the Northern Hemisphere, thinking they are birds for a time. To them, the clouds look woolen. The sky is a pasture of parading sheep with no weight to them. These witless, wingless creatures. Even flightless birds have wings strapped to them. They have only to learn to use what has languished into desuetude. They have only to flap them fast enough when time comes to sail off a cliff at predator's approach. But this world spins too fast and they are not in time, not in time. Late past all hope.

Sometimes I wonder if this planet will ever tire of turning, if it too will take a lamb's leap somewhere, far beyond its orbit, if it will fall into a puddle of mud and stand in the spray of a garden hose. I should like to see that, but I don't expect it. My life is halfway over now, if not more so, and this world is already an old one. It is only young life that springs high enough to puncture clouds of wool. It is only Jesus and lambs and birds that have taught themselves to fly. Spring is the youngest season, while I have always favored autumn.

In the chill of an April autumn morning, we left Queenstown to take a helicopter somewhere fewer people lived among a greater preponderance of sheep. We took a helicopter because my credit card had just room enough and I too felt like springing. Because whatever else I am, I'm no flightless bird. I'm not dead yet. Daddy, do you hear me? Do you hear my little lamb voice over the helicopter wings? A thrash of sabers through air sheared close to the belly.

The man who carried our bags to our hotel room in Wellington stood no more than five feet tall. The top of his head was even with my shoulders. He had dark, rippling hair and cobalt eyes the size of lakes seen from a helicopter's height. They were lakes shimmering with desire when he looked first into my face and level with the slope of my breasts hung snug inside my sweater. When he closed the door, my husband said I gave that little man a hard-on, and I told him to go fuck himself. Because I had not seen such bodies of water casting their glow on me for too long a time.

Unlike Jesus, sheep cannot walk through walls of any kind. They cannot see out of buckets either with no holes punched through them, and any farmer's herd has only one ram, with all the ewes to his lonesome. Taller by a head than his harem, he surveys his options while his testicles scrape thedandelions clean of pollen. He is the only sheep tall enough to stretch and eat the apples hanging from the lowest branches.

One morning when I was nine or ten or eleven, our ram's bellows woke me from dreaming. He butted his head, covered in a plastic bucket, against a tree trunk. The bucket I had left beside the ladder, full of apples the night before. With his hunger sated, he now saw nothing but the bucket's blackness. We scrambled our eggs and fried our bacon without hurry, however. We lavished our toast with jelly, laughing the louder the longer he yawped in panic. Even darkness can be funny when you look on at a sheep gone blind like the doll you've long lost track of.

Once our lambs turned three months old, my dad sawed off their horn stumps to keep them from growing long and turning against us. He held each lamb between his legs while clamping shut its jaw. And when he was finished, I waved the saw still with blood at its teeth in the wind. I made it ululate and harmonized with its wail as best I could, singing in some new language. I may have been sounding Maori incantations for all I knew different, begging the gods to accept my offering, though I never knew where the little horns were kept. Whatever spirits I invoked or didn't, my voice ached with so much unmet beauty, echoing off the barn we had just painted, that my dad ripped the saw from my hand and hung it out of reach.

In Rotorua, we ate sushi in a strip mall. Afterward, we walked toward the hot springs, passing a man with ashen skin and no body below his waist. His rib cage supported too reedy a neck for his head not to keep dropping from its weight. Propped in a wheelchair outside a store selling liquor and cigarettes, the man looked at me with eyes whose whites were blank as newly shorn sheep skin in the sign's phosphorescence. They shone with too stark a whiteness for so late in the evening. And as he gazed into my pupils' widening darkness, I saw his irises were too blue a blue as well, that they glowed with a watchfulness I hoped would fade come daylight. I turned my head away from him, inhaling sulfur from the mud in which I soon would kick my legs like scissors through glue.

In the hot springs, I wore the $100 bathing suit and swam through pools of increasing warmth. I spent the longest time in the hottest and overlooked a sky teeming with stars so numerous I thought there might be enough, that stars should have their predators too, as glow worms also must. Inside the mud pool not long afterward, I sat beside my husband on a low cement step and felt my lower body cool into an emptiness. The mud concealed all my body below my ribs, which expanded and contracted without my consent. I could see only the part of me too that might survive in a wheelchair on this continent. Had all the longing died out of me like headlights at an ignition's click, the whites of my eyes too might still be very white, much too white to serve any purpose. Had that which glowed blue inside me as any glow worm not been below my navel and instead inside my iris.

Jesus is a lamb, common as rain come springtime, abundant as feathers on any flightless bird. And lambs leap high in the air as they can manage but soon fall to the ground, where wild dogs wait for wingless creatures. When Easter too comes to New Zealand, the leaves have all but fallen and the lambs are lambs no more. Too tired to leap with their wool grown heavy, they masticate blonde grasses lining the luge tracks. They watch endless cataracts of a species all too common ascend the skies in the funicular before disappearing into the lake beyond. They see toboggans meet gray waters while they stay high on a hill, knowing no one will bury them here now.

The Etymology of Honey

Eating Thanksgiving in Savannah, drinking white zinfandel while seated across from a couple from Prague who have since moved to Ottawa, God only knows the reason, was not something I ever really wanted. We came here, though, because I bought plane tickets to another city so the holiday would seem less lonesome. And as this man and this woman kept speaking, I scraped the flat of my shoe against the grain of the carpet. I smudged a vine leaf into a jellyfish as they talked of losing sight of each other in the snow while walking to their mailbox a quarter mile from their home.

As snow began clotting on their eyelashes and they watched each other dissolve halfway down the driveway into whiteness, I tried to forget my name, soft as sunlight filtering through coral, a lambent gaslight glow that might be no light at all in an Ottawan snowsquall. I didn't repeat it either when they asked but pretended I didn't hear. I fixed my eyes on the fire unlit inside the hearth, a cold charcoal womb.

As the womb chilled and hardened, my breath began escaping out the ventricles of my heart, as if I were a bee instead of a woman, with no lungs at all. The air within didn't bother snaking out my nose and mouth as it used to do, pulsing on its voyage to the mantle, where a fern waved, flaunting its spore show. And this, I thought, was progress, breathing without a mouth and directly through my internal organs. Becoming each moment less of a person. Almost a flying insect.

Sure as tadpoles shedding gills for lungs to come, I felt my sense of self loosen as I sat refusing to utter my name to the couple seated on the opposite couch. I swam among silence that was a warmth of its own. No one here would light the fire, but I felt myself step into its flames all the same, because God only wants you once he has burnt all the apple skin off your face. No one gets burnt walking over hot coals except for on the balls of their feet, and you're not doing anything for appearances' sake. You're clipping your toenails close as you can to the cuticle. Until there's nothing left to paint.

God wants to see your eyes and nothing else anyway. One extant eyelash spoils the whole effect. God won't heal you, but he'll like you better this way. And even inside the fire incinerating your ego, it is there always, this aversion to a benign people living in a benign country just north of Niagara Falls where the earth recedes into nothingness. A people with a way of saying "snow" you like no more than you do pubic hair that circles your bathtub drain and refuses to disappear down its hole. God only knows where all that water goes.

It is the things that cling that keep you from falling fast asleep, that are too lovely for too short a time, clinging the harder for being so fleeting. Brown leaves pendent from a tomato plant. The quivering of a butterfly's breath. Honey thinning as it falls from a spoon with a dented stem. And that is enough, is all in fact. The suspension. A hive hanging from a baobab hanging from a planet spinning the same as a ball of lint among an ink-spilled emptiness. A planet roiling with desire as yet unmet, in one ellipse after another around some stationary star burning past all comprehension. A planet hung by nothing except a single thread, thinner than a bee's spittle, from what kind of ceiling fixture I cannot begin to imagine. Just because you are falling too doesn't mean you can like every people and country under the sun bobbing in the firmament. You've still got your prejudices so long as your hair grows longer each minute. So long as you've got your eyelashes, you've got your limits.

Fortunately, life doesn't require your liking, only a few short breaths, some in, some out, in a certain sequence. And this you allow because you have long been sure you are living more than one life at a time as it is. And it's hard to stop breathing. This life, it carries you. It holds you aloft until its arms grow heavy, which takes longer than you think, pushing you closer to the sun than is really good for your complexion.

You are also busy enough in other lifetimes to sit for a moment on a faded floral-print couch in this. You are stretched thin as a starfish splayed on snow with all this living, which is why you've started taking naps. You sleep most of these silken Savannah afternoons in which there is nothing to do except shift your weight on a sewer lid, tilting its flat head with first this foot then that, rocking it back and forth to test whether you'll fall down a manhole where you're pretty sure there are no men at all.

Yet you are in love, always in love. Even here, sitting before the unlit fire, shuddering at the Ottawan cold by way of Prague, you circle the drain like lost pubic hair, but you don't fall down it. You give so much of yourself—your beautiful breadfruit breasts and your sweet inner thigh sap to men cruising different dimensions, almost colliding though never, no, not yet—you have no love for Canadians left. And you can't finish your glass of wine, which is much too sweet without even a trace of honey some bee has just vomited to dry inside its hive.

Exhume Egyptian mummies embalmed thousands of years before this and all is dank, dark rot. All save their jardinières of honey, manuka or avocado, maybe mint or sage. The sage, though, is only a plant, never a wise person you might entreat for guidance, and the honey sits entombed, wasted. Honey, your namesake, originating from the Greek. You rub your fists inside your eyelids, sending messages to yourself traveling through other incarnations.

You almost remember beginning your life as a nymph, feeding Zeus honey rather than milk as a baby. From you, the bees learned to alchemize nectar, so it's little wonder you've never wanted offspring. Not when you've already reared a race of gods, not when the amber-colored blood flowing through your veins and out your tear ducts never sours. Not in the dankest sepulcher. Not when you yourself are too sweet for any bees to sting, over so many lifetimes. You could run barefoot in the dandelion grass all summer.

You're having no children because children can no longer survive on honey alone, not since the gods left you to feed on flounder the last Thursday of November. You don't order turkey because the flounder is the house specialty, recommended by the waiter. The fish is served on the bone, drizzled with an apricot sauce that hardens into candy. Your providing days are over and you are no longer a nymph, a minor female deity. You are drinking wine in Savannah in the company of Canadians because you can think of nothing better.

The time has passed for deciding to do something different, to be either a child to parents long dead or birth children of your own to die upon too early. The time for deciding is at an end, and there is nothing left except to fly to Savannah from Chicago the day before Thanksgiving because you and your husband have never been and the earth there might be warmer. Though it is not, not enough to justify the trip. Temperatures are twenty degrees cooler here than average, so you light the fireplace in your room come evening. You fall asleep as the flames heave their hollow breaths. You cough in your sleep and wake exhausted.

You left Chicago a day earlier than your husband to explore the city without him, and you know he would do the same had he the option. His boss, though, will only give him so many days for vacation while you work on a freelance basis. You may have long lost your nymph wings, but when you can fly away on a pair made from steel a day early, you do, always. With your seatbelt buckled low and tight across your hips, you cross your legs and jut your knee hard against the seat in front of you, into an old man's coccyx.

When you land, you tour no mansions but read a novel through a thunderstorm instead. You read while trying not to love a man you'll never see again, a man you met in a bookstore whose pale blue eyes followed you as you browsed the mystery section two weeks before this.

You browsed but don't read mysteries, because they supply answers at their end. And to answers you prefer questions, mysteries where the mystery remains, though to questions you prefer kissing. Still you trace the raised gold lettering along the books' spinal columns. Your fingers cling the longer to cursive names so you won't have to lift your finger until the name's last letter. Yet this is something you can do only in bookstores. You can always read at home beneath the covers or at the kitchen table for light that's brighter.

While there, however, you can strum a thousand spines like a Grecian lyre. You play well enough by vibration, making no music, because even when sound goes there is always the touch of the instrument. Lips always tell more when they're not speaking, so better to speed the spines' circulation. And tracing successive nom de plumes, your forefinger grows a little stiff, though the rosebush between your legs begins blooming. His eyes stay with your index finger, and that is all that matters for the moment. The moment hangs, though, thick as slow-falling honey, which no one may ever taste besides the bees and bees alone.

Trying not to love men you know only by their sidelong gazes while you read during thunderstorms has become what you do the day before Thanksgiving in lieu of baking pumpkin pie or making casserole. Not that you ever liked casserole for starters. Not that you can't buy pie at the grocery. And on the whole you prefer it, this languorous bid at nonloving at which you will never succeed, though if you did it would make little difference. You can eat all the honey you please from an Egyptian sarcophagus, yet you can't bring back the person buried within it.

The man in the bookstore was half bear. He wore an ursine sweater with an autumn beard hiding half his face. He was your same height, and he asked your name then repeated it to himself with a smile you couldn't see but sensed behind the bear's bristle. If you saw him without his beard come summer, you might not recognize him. And once the fire burns you completely, once you return to Chicago from Savannah, he won't know you either.

As you coax your love into nonlove, you might not recognize yourself, without any hair after all, only burnt patches for skin brittle at the edges. You walk closer to the fire and pluck an eyelash. You squint with the pain of detaching it. You unwrap yourself from the robe you found hanging inside the closet and sit before the flames with your legs arranged in the lotus position. A chill at your back from the open window. Sweat pooling at your rump and running between your toe crevices.

There is too much room inside this room. It is as desolate as the inside of an atom. More space in this one Savannah bedroom than inside your whole apartment, where you let honey drip down the sides of the jar, shaped like a skep. When you lift it, the jar takes part of the cupboard paint with it, accreting a larger sheath each time you decide to sweeten a cup of tea. The jar resists spiritual evolution, embroils itself in further ego enhancement— cloaking itself with white cupboard paint, clown makeup for all intents and purposes—while you are the cupboard, which may and may not be made of driftwood, washed ashore from a shipwreck. You are the one who strips the cupboard of its whitest layer of skin by not wiping down the honey jar, almost on purpose, because the damage is already done and what's a little more lost paint to your landlord?

At breakfast next morning, the cook's face registers surprise to see you seated alone at a table for four and facing a pineapple tilted against a window. The pineapple is a symbol of fertility, you remember from a college course in Rome, though maybe it was a pinecone—all those seeds blown open by a furnace or fire in the forest. Two other couples sit pouring cream into their coffee at opposite ends of the dining room while you eat in the kitchen and watch him—his name is Mario, and his eyebrows hover at variant latitudes—fry bacon, poach eggs, cream spinach, and pour milk into a tiny pitcher you could balance on your palm because you don't drink cream, only whole milk, with your coffee, every morning.

You apologize to him for being particular, though have no intention of drinking cream either. You aren't really sorry, only trying to be polite, though the Canadians already have that base covered, the Canadians who only laughed when they asked your name three times and you stayed silent. He asks what's on the day's agenda, and you tell him that you'll likely walk, eat, and read, the same as you'd do at home were you not working.

If Mario continues asking questions, you're prepared to be honest, but you don't begin to tell him you're already tired from a night spent trying not to love someone you hardly even met in a bookstore where you bought nothing to read. You don't muster the courage to confess you'll sleep a good half the day wearing a summer dress it's much too cold to wear outside today, that mystery novels are more mysterious when you leave them on the shelf.

So long as you're awake, today you'll live as though there's another thunderstorm brewing, even though the sky is clear and blue. Mario tells you to have some fun, however. He curls the side of his mouth up into a snail shell spiral, saying you're too pretty not to. He examines you, squaring his gaze over his eyeglass frames. He advises you to watch out for Southern gentlemen, because not all deserve the name. Some are only horny toads, he says, while flipping a slice of bacon lean as a lizard with its tail foreshortened.

This morning you looked hard into the mirror, harder than you wanted, and saw fresh evidence the nymph has long since fled the coop, because all along the nymph may have really been a chicken. The truth, of course, is the nymph hasn't been around since Mount Olympus. This burning up of beauty doesn't have much further to go if it ever existed. Only the cook is 45 or 50, and of all the women in the bed and breakfast you are perhaps the one most shaped like an amphora ancient Egyptians slept with in their coffins. The only one here alone for certain.

The panicked yelp of a dog outside, and you laugh as Mario hands you a bowl of granola with strawberries sliced into symmetrical mouse heart halves splayed over dried cherries. Smooth as their skin is, the strawberries' seeds resemble large pores, green and gaping, hungry for dispersal in the soil's underbelly. Another fertility symbol here—or perhaps the opposite—because strawberries reproduce asexually, each so sweet it requires nothing but wind to spawn its offspring, like the fern spores falling onto the rug in the living room. Strawberries don't long for other strawberries. And once your sense of self evaporates entirely, once desire flakes off you like a poisoned chrysalis, you too will be a strawberry, at least metaphorically.

Your pores will be larger, yet they will be your only holes for a stranger to enter. You'll have no such thing as a vagina, your largest lacuna, better sealed with rubber as if you were a Barbie. Your skin will be redder, your shape rounder, and you won't be able to wiggle your toes, because you'll have no feet either. No one's eyes will follow your index finger to the mystery section once you metamorphose into an asexual fruit. You will be pink pineal flawlessness. Sliceable and sour if picked too soon.

Pouring you more coffee, Mario says his dog has had puppies. A litter of six, three boys and three girls, imagine the burden. Like the Brady Bunch, you think but keep silent, remembering Mr. and Mrs. Brady had their children from previous marriages, making Greg and Marsha's sexual attraction less creepy though not worth mentioning. His dog, Perseus, Mario continues, smothered the three girls within their first few hours of life, leaving Bobby, Peter, and Greg alone, incest no more a question. You gasp, and he walks back to his skillet, saying that was nature's prerogative. Perseus knew she couldn't rear six children, so she killed the weakest, sitting on them until their breath died out of their lungs. Six lungs for three little girls, a perfect, useless number. Does Mario get to take his share of leftovers home from the kitchen? you ask to change the subject. All the uneaten strawberries, he says, red as flame tips resting on the window ledge with the curtains open. Ideal puppy food for three young virgins.

Reaching for a pot of honey stacked on a macedoine of grape and orange jellies, you read the label, "Pure honey, honey!" Your mom never said a thing to you about Zeus or his diet as a baby or the nymph who fed him, and you still can't quite forgive her ignorance. It was almost as if she didn't want to know the kinds of things you would do with your forefinger in bookstores once she had left you here to your loneliness. You can't help thinking she would have made a good Canadian. Dead eight years, she's equally impervious to cold now too. She should have eaten more honey while she could, you think yet cannot tell her.

Stepping outside, you zip your coat up to your neck. Walking through a cemetery, you see a woman smoking and wearing a red sock hat. Beside her a Boxer is standing on a grave, flat and raised as tall as a coffee table. Split by a tree root, the grave looks a hundred years old if not more, and you smile to yourself as the dog's eyes follow a squirrel racing up a tree trunk. Below the headstone lie the remains of a man or woman, probably a slave owner and, the inscription reads, a philanthropist also. Someone who could afford a headstone five times the size of your parents'. Someone whose inner thigh sap may have been as rich and honeyed as your own.

The woman drops her cigarette on the cement and calls her dog to follow when she sees you approach. A tiny fire still smolders at tobacco's tip, and when you pass the grave you grind out the light into darkness, scattering its ash into a slate-colored bruise across the sidewalk. It looks as if you've just hurt someone, though you don't know whom.

No one knows why Egyptians buried their dead with their arms crossed over their rib cages. There are theories, but no one knows for certain.

Perhaps they were easier to wrap without their arms extended like branches. Perhaps they were folded in prayer, waiting to meet the gods in a pious posture. Yet you think—you almost, with your fists pressed hard against your eyelids, know as fact—it is because death is a cold dwelling place. And it's stealing on you here, in the Savannah chill, beside the cloven headstone. You have left your gloves in your room and cross your arms over your chest to keep warm, waiting for no god of any name.

Tomorrow, Thanksgiving, will be warmer. And while you will not be thankful, you will be more comfortable walking out of doors, far from any fire. You will hold your husband's hand as you shuffle between parking meters dotting the riverfront like talismans, demanding coins to keep watch on evil dressed as Southern gentlemen. Were you as sweet as your mother had been, you would drop spare change inside each of them, change saved in a purple pouch she kept in her glove compartment without any gloves inside it. Only you're nothing like your mother, not any longer. Your honey-feeding days are over. You're closing your eyes waiting for the big burn and nothing more.

Behind your eyelids, your eyes are still wide, wide open, astonished by the veins' filigree inside the skin skirting your lashes. Here you can still see the eyes that followed you through the whodunits. You know the culprit without reading a word of any manuscript. You, not the butler, did it, and you'll have nothing but hell to pay for it. Hell, though, is what you came here for, a day earlier than you needed.

Weeping Virgin

Our first morning in Seville and for miles he trailed my shadow at a distance. He was walking slowly as an old, arthritic man, I knew, on purpose. Yet this is the problem with striking your husband outside a shop selling spices. This is the problem with inflicting violence while the Virgen de la Macarena cries glass teardrops glued below her eye sockets. No one notices those who carry her are weeping for the love denied them in private. They walk a straight path regardless, their shoulders gone crooked with emotion, as the crowd diverges for a statue blessed with anguish beyond them.

Even now, months later, I'm still not quite forgiven. I can tell by the way my husband scours my back with our soap's sprigs of rosemary, abrading my skin into a terrible smoothness blind to its own beauty. I prefer to shower alone while shaving my legs. Only he likes time spent with me naked when we're not fucking. When I scrape my knee and it bleeds, he shows me how to hold the razor, delicately as the stem of a flower begun wilting.

My behavior is becoming so erratic, though, you can hardly trust me to hold a razor blade. You have to take the blow I struck in context, he told me. I scratched at my face as he was talking, trying to detach the mole from my cheek, needing to hurt some supple part of me. I had only wanted to smell the spices packed in burlap bags, to live with a certain sensuality despite being married, to climax merely from looking at the yellow buildings with their gleaming tile tapestries. Here in the cult of the weeping virgin, I'd grown tired of his old man's walking.

A vagina is a tear in the skin of a female adult or baby, a fabric slit for buttons lost in the laundry. What lies inside is almost too delicate to consider before ten in the evening, when the Spanish just sit down to eat—all those tiny eggs with shells cracking so easily yet still might become another person.

But a hole's a hole, and there's no use threading any needle to repair the damage. As a woman, you must learn to live with it the same as a phantom leg still strung with nerve endings, to walk while feeling mostly empty. The poor Virgin Mary never let anybody explore her own sweet crevice, wet with everything but longing. All she ever did was pee out of it in times with less toilet paper, I'm guessing.

Yet if there is a rip in the fabric of the universe, as some scientists speculate, a tear through which time and space can dissolve into nothing, it is also a gateway to the body of a woman who birthed all these planets looking like heads freed from their bodies. The conception, though, was immaculate because there was never a large enough phallus to fill her opening. Otherwise, all the universe would be sticky with semen, the air we're breathing always humid. The Virgin Mary wasn't so special is what I'm saying. Had she had sex once, she'd have faded from all memory.

We say "tags," the Spanish "stickers," at least when they speak English. A woman with eyes the color of emeralds dusted with cardamom or some spice equally aromatic was the second to remind me my sticker was showing from my dress, which was shorter than necessary, I knew from looks several men had given me. The first person to tell me my sticker had fallen outside my dress was a man who watched me pour my coffee inside our hotel lobby. Then later that evening, I left my husband with a plate of half-eaten aubergine drizzled with honey after we'd quarreled the second time since morning. I'd forgotten to use the toilet at the restaurant while running away from him down a dark, reflective alley.

This time, I didn't strike him. I only started crying, forgetting I already had such a large tear inside of me, that I could drain myself of only so much liquid before becoming completely empty. A few minutes after I left him waiting to pay the check, I was walking toward the ladies' room at the far corner of a courtyard roped from public entry. A woman came and asked me what I was doing inside a private institute for gifted children, as the sign clearly stated. Looking into her face, I wanted to ask her what spice her eyes were wearing. I wanted to ask her, though, in English, because I speak no Spanish, when she told me to tuck in my sticker, please.

The toilet seat in the restroom she let me use so long as I went quickly was wet when I sat down without looking. It was the spilled urine of some child supplied with intelligence beyond me. Leaving, I saw the same woman smoking, leaning against a wall near a playground's entrance. The wall was spray-painted with a tree, and she stood against its trunk. The tree, though, had also started flying. Its roots were turning into flames, poised to propel it into outer space, a haze of green and yellow spray paint. Behind the cigarette smoke clouding her face, I watched her eyes dart and run away from me. Still they smelled of something cooking, something she refused to share with me. For dinner, I had eaten only a few slices of aubergine and was starving. More than eat, however, I wanted to ride that arboreal spaceship into another forested galaxy.

As I walked on, I watched men and women avert their eyes from my face, blotched in pale peach patches from crying. My patchworked face had begun unraveling, and its seams were showing. I'd become repulsive here in a city where even the Virgen de la Macarena is a dark and olive-skinned beauty. The Spanish avoid displays of suffering unless you're a lifelong virgin whose son was flagellated in public.

Stores in Seville selling aprons flaring like flamenco dresses at their bottoms and small matadors sculpted from porcelain keep late hours while most bars see few customers until early morning. So I walked inside a few shops after leaving the school for gifted children. At first, I thought I'd buy some pen and paper to explain my reasons for killing myself with razors once I recrossed the Atlantic. I decided, though, eventually to write no goodbye letter to those who would only accuse me of being selfish.

I bought myself a small wooden box instead. Two tiles form its lid, tiles looking like those flanking all Seville conservatories, while its clasp resembles a diadem better fit for some sovereign. I have no idea what I'll put inside it now that I've decided to keep living. It may always be a space for nothing on a dresser crowded as it is with small bottles of perfume my mom once gave me. I never spray any of them on my pulse points as she showed me, only twist off their caps and smell them before I fall asleep, as if they're laced with laudanum or something with equally magical properties.

When I returned to the hotel a little after 11:30, I told my husband while washing my face that my life would be over quickly. Death solves all problems, I still wholly believe. Life, though, wants to keep living, feeding an endless greed. Its appetite is the same as that of a woman whose hole never closes. Life has no religion. It only wants to keep fucking. Yet when you're dressed and done making love, ready to go eat, your tag should not be showing. Because you're not a virgin, you should not be weeping.

Madrid was all my mom ever saw of this country. The man she came to see—the man whose name eludes me, so seldom did she say it—she hardly even mentioned in the story she told nearly each Thanksgiving. Instead, it was the priests who made a deeper impression. Yet before she met either one of them, she'd known a Spaniard, an exchange student, back in college. She'd made plans to meet him in the medieval castle where he still lived with his parents, a castle fitted with modern plumbing. Only she left his address and phone number back home in another coat pocket. She'd also brought too little money to eat anything except day-old bread and cheese. Prior to this as well as after, she did very little traveling.

On what was her one trip to Europe, taken in her early twenties, she went with a friend who rode the subway with her throughout an entire evening. They'd left the hostel where someone had rummaged through their luggage, taken precious money. They had stopped speaking. While her friend sat silent, my mom starting talking to a priest. He was praying a rosary with

56

beads looking like opals, the same as the earrings she gave me for my eighteenth birthday, the same as those I later lost one summer when swimming.

While in Spain for less than a week, my mom was still a virgin as well as a devout Catholic, something she never stopped being. If she were going to be talking to any stranger, she naturally found herself a priest. In the course of conversation, she told him she had lost the telephone number of a certain boyfriend—not her lover—though of the two monikers I prefer the latter and don't mind substituting it now for her. The priest, as it happens, knew both the boy and his father. Their orange grove was legendary, he ravished. The oranges were all shipped to England to make marmalade, however.

A few days after the priest gave her the address and phone number, she met the Spaniard and refused his offer of marriage. Here I always stopped her, wanting her to elaborate, even embroider. Each time she refused me, saying only that Spanish men made poor husbands. They left their wives home weeping while probing other women's tears and ripping them wider open. All she ever wanted was for him to show her the castle with plumbing.

After she met the man she came for only ostensibly, only to see but not be loved by him, she was still short of money. She had enough, though, to keep riding the subway, where she met another priest. This was the point in the story when she always started laughing and I grew restless for her to finish. She told him she had only enough money to eat once a day, when he gave her a couple hundred dollars, which amounted to much more in the 1960s. He wanted her to take the train to Lourdes, however, before flying back home from Paris. No need to repay him, he insisted. If she didn't humor him, he said the Blessed Virgin would weep for her unborn children.

I told her this sounded like a threat, but she said I misread his intention. He only wanted her to seek the Virgin Mother's protection on our behalf, as if we were endangered several years out from conception.

Protection from what? I asked her. From sin, she said, as if that were an explanation. As if even had the virgin kept me from slapping my husband, I'd ever care much for living once she refused my mom's prayers for healing. I don't expect much, however, of an old virgin who herself looks none too happy.

Our last day in Seville, I walked up the middle aisle as the priest began his sermon. I walked up while mass was in progress to see the famous statue of the weeping virgin whose glass tears glimmered like jewels. The priest frowned at me and looked to see if my sticker was showing, so I walked back and stayed standing near the baptistery. I rubbed the feet of a statue of Jesus in imitation of some other women. And I began softly crying when I scratched at his big toe, as if to relieve some itching from poison ivy. Itch an irritant, however, and it only grows the more irritating.

I scratched at Jesus' feet but asked neither him nor Mary for anything, because my worst wound lies beyond all healing. I was born with it as a baby, and it only widens when I stretch my legs. Every other woman I know has one just the same, and I don't see them lying like I do on park benches, almost writhing, while homeless men come closer with their carts full of winter clothing smelling of feces.

And as we left the church where the saddest statue all in the world resides, a line was lengthening to buy tickets for the lottery.

Although Mary remained a virgin all her days, whether Joseph ever wriggled his finger around inside her remains a possibility. Perhaps at times she felt something where God tore her asunder. I wonder only because my own hole is throbbing. Because this is the real reason the people of Seville have seen me cry in public. Sew it shut and I promise I'll hit no one who might still its pulsing.

My mom told the story of the two Spanish priests so often I eventually stopped hearing. The trip to Lourdes felt a needless departure from the main story, because at the time she was perfectly healthy. She could have stilled her own pulsing. She could have lived all her life in Spain if she'd only wanted, giving birth to me in a castle smelling of orange groves rather than a farm in Indiana, giving me better skin as well as genetics. Instead, she took the train to rural France as bidden, leaving the closest she'd ever come to royalty.

The Real Alcázar serves as the Seville residence of the Spanish royal family, though much of it is open to the public. Originally a Moorish citadel, the name means "courtyard of the maidens," a reference to the Moors' demand for a hundred annual virgins. The holes of virgins are tighter than those of other women and so provide more pleasure to those who enter, or so goes the logic. They tire more easily, though, and bleed from their hymen, so a man might require more for satisfaction.

The gardens of the Real Alcázar abound with the same orange trees you see all across the city, and by the time we reached them we'd walked for hours and I'd grown famished. I decided to pick one but had to run to build momentum to jump and snatch it. My husband reminded me they were too bitter to eat. They were smaller than those we bought at the grocery but less sweet. How do you know? I asked him. Well he'd read it somewhere, obviously. I had read the same passage in the same guidebook as he, but reading is a limited way of knowing. Better to taste, I said, happy my body could disagree.

When I peeled back the rind, flung it in the bushes, and ate half the orange at once, I told him it wasn't as bitter as he thought it would be. He tried some and agreed. We picked two more and put them in our pockets then ate them after our tapas later that evening.

My mom often said she dreamt of returning to Spain and seeing the Virgen de la Macarena paraded through Seville's streets during Holy Week— she would have traveled to Andalusia if she'd only had more money from another priest. The statue, though, is not as lovely as you might imagine, I have tried telling her posthumously. One cheek has sustained damage from some apostate who struck the virgin's face with a wine bottle whose wine was only half finished. The statue itself is wooden, and the virgin's hair is human, meaning that which looks most natural on her decays most quickly.

In addition to practicing abstinence, the Virgin Mary's body never perished, from cancer, for instance. Angels carried her bodily into Heaven according to Catholic doctrine while she still breathed, so that in a world of spirits she remains the only body, so that her urine must filter into the rain. People worship her nevertheless, especially in this city, loving her more for crying in public, something that only makes me enemies.

When I was eight years old, I told my mom that a crustacean's blood was the color of the ocean. I told her because in school I had just learned this, because the fact felt so necessary. I pulled a bag of crayfish out from our freezer then thawed and cut one open to show her it looked nothing like that flowing through our own arteries. I watched her jaw open at the revelation and suddenly knew that she knew nothing. It was as I suspected. I sighed and realized I would have to teach myself everything.

You learn nothing either by praying the rosary, something I discovered at roughly the same age as I committed the crustacean anatomy to memory. My mom told me to pray the rosary before I fell asleep, to ask forgiveness from a woman whose body was never buried. Yet I didn't feel sorry for anything. I'd hit my sister once and bitten her leg so a day later the teeth marks were still showing, though even that never made me feel guilty. I had so much to learn, so many facts between the earth and moon and fluids escaping the tear inside my body. Still I knew enough not to rely on priests for money.

In the tapas bar where old men kept tabs with chalk they soaked in water then wrote down on the counter, I went blind for several minutes. My dress revealed ample cleavage, so I kept my coat on once we met by accident a Welshman we'd spoken with at a flamenco performance. I didn't want to remind him of the large tear inside of me, one he could fill if only technically.

The room grew warmer with each person who walked in, and that day I had hardly eaten. When I drank a glass of wine too quickly, I toppled backward, slicing part of my wrist open on a beer glass I shattered in the process. The blood, I noticed when my eyes started working again, ran red instead of blue. I was startled by the crimson color that widened across the floor like a river pouring itself into the ocean. If I ever shaved my wrists in the shower, I would stain the tub almost too vivid a color. I would make a mess for my husband, one that would only remind him I was a human rather than crustacean each time he lathered.

And as I listened to people wonder aloud whether I was conscious or had gotten a concussion, my husband said my eyes were opened wider than looked natural. I never stared with such intensity as when all the world went invisible.

The Virgen de la Macarena keeps watch over all Spain's matadors, we learned while taking a tour of a bullfighting museum the next morning. In 1912, José Ortega weighted the statue with five emerald brooches, soliciting further intercession and acclaim in his profession. Yet eight years later, a bull gored him through the aorta. The wooden virgin then wore black as a sign of the city's mourning, the only time in Seville's history she changed her clothes to anyone's knowledge. José Ortega, though, was sexy. He was greatly missed by the more devout women of the city.

When trying to understand why the Virgen de la Macarena is weeping, orthodox thinking points to her son's crucifixion. Jesus, though, is risen if you ask anyone who believes he has saved them. Her tears are specious then as well as easily broken. The truth is she's crying for other reasons. Her son was born to save the world, she was told from the beginning. She gave birth as predicted to a living deity—any suffering she knew was fleeting—so hush there, sweetie. You're not the only one hurting. Behind her tears, in Spain you'll notice, she is always slightly smiling.

The Hail Mary implores her to act as our intermediary, to beg her son to forgive us our iniquities. Jesus meanwhile sits beside her, luminescing and likely bored with the monotony, tired of doing nothing for all eternity except forgiving. So there is only one cause left for her continued sorrow. The Blessed Virgin will be a virgin always. The tear between her legs was made for nothing but exits.

Mary's mother, Ann, was canonized solely for birthing the woman who conceived without having a phallus probe her lowest opening. Ann appears nowhere in the Bible or Qur'an, but in Apocrypha only, according to which she thought herself infertile but became pregnant when considered well advanced in age in times when people died much younger on average. She reportedly had three children from husbands numbering the same, and she named each Mary for reasons beyond reckoning. Ecclesiastical authorities, however, later pronounced this as spurious. Ann had just the one baby. There can be only one weeping virgin, unless you're a heretic, though the name has remained so common.

My husband's mother's name was Mary, though she died of cancer years before I met her son in a bookstore cafe. The chicken pox scar above the gap between my eyebrows has the same shape and occupies the same position as her own once did, and he says it frightened him from the beginning, as if she were returning in a different body. I have seen pictures of her, however, and bear her no resemblance. I was born while she was still living. I also have no wish to mother my husband. I cover my own small scar with bangs falling low across my forehead.

After I struck my husband, his face grew ugly to me, though mine is none too pretty. I suggested he have his hair cut after I finished apologizing.

We needed something to distract us from the hand I'd flung and through which I'd wretched some poison. And as I sat flipping through magazines of Spanish celebrities and my husband looked at his own face in the mirror reflected at me from a distance, the barber stood between us.

The barber in the opera whose title my husband repeated throughout the day's remainder, saying he had met the barber of Seville and isn't that funny, is no barber at all, only a factotum, something I tried inserting into the hilarity. Figaro pretends to be a hair stylist to protect a pair of lovers, of whom the male, Count Almaviva, is his employer. Rosina and Almaviva manage to fool Rosina's guardian, who wants to marry her as well, though only for her dowry. The haircut takes places halfway through the opera, when Figaro botching the job elates the audience as well as keeps the play rolling. The guardian is old and ugly while Almaviva is young and handsome as the Spaniard my mom could have married in the 1960s.

After he had his hair cut in a style we both agreed made him look a little like Morrissey, we rode a carousel. A street performer wearing a Spiderman costume began circling us as we spun around an axis wrapped in ceramic ribbons tied to nothing. He kept pace with us then started heckling, Hey sexy! We could see his hardened penis through his spandex sheathing, his abdomen strung with spider web veins. When the ride ended and my husband took my hand, he blamed me for wearing too tight of clothes. At least I wasn't wearing spandex, I said, which showed everything.

If my mom spoke more of Lourdes after she left Spain along with a man who could have fucked her into an outer orbit, I cannot tell you any more of the story. She never finished it to my memory, many times as she told it. I also doubt there's much worth telling. She brought back a vial of water from Bernadette's famous stream, a vial I later emptied into the sink when I was six or seven. I filled it with two half bottles of nail polish, mixing them into a color I thought nicer than each looked separately. I saw a picture of the Virgin Mary weeping on the front of what looked like tap water to me, a vial imprinted with gold lacquer I scraped away with an emery board while I watched TV. My mom teared up in a hot rage that quickly softened into instruction on the love that came from a woman living in heaven with a body whose tears were waters of healing.

Mary appeared to Bernadette Soubirous as an apparition according to legend. The virgin made a request of this peasant girl in person, asking her to build a chapel beside a brook whose waters could cure those who were suffering. Mary appeared to her for two consecutive weeks each evening, with a yellow rose resting on each foot, identifying herself only as the Immaculate Conception, telling Bernadette to drink the spring's water and bathe there as well. After which, witnesses confirmed, the mud permeating the waters vanished, allowing pilgrims passing through airport security to bring samples home more easily.

Bernadette died at the age of 35, my same age as of writing. Her body, church documents attest, has been exhumed three times. Thirty years after she stopped breathing, photographs showed her body to lie unaltered, though the rosary and crucifix she was buried with had rusted badly. As further relics were taken, the presiding physician, a Dr. Comte, recorded the following: "What struck me during this examination, of course, was the state of perfect preservation of the skeleton, the fibrous tissues of the muscles (still supple and firm), of the ligaments, and of the skin, and above all the totally unexpected state of the liver after 46 years." Maybe it's just me, but to my ears he sounds a little turned on by Bernadette's dead body.

Perhaps the reason I never heard what happened once my mom left Madrid for the French backcountry was because I felt Bernadette was the daughter she really wanted instead of me. But no such luck, Mommy. Were I to kill myself before my next birthday, we would die at the same age. Only you won't be here to acknowledge the congruity.

Chemists who have examined the composition of Lourdes' waters have noted no differences from that we drink everywhere else across the planet. It is potable and wet with no special mineral properties. Were you to visit there in summer, you'd have no chance to swim there either, because the crowds are endless. Once you reach the spring, you'd only be rushed through to make way for those with more manifest maladies. There are also few public toilets, while you're prohibited from contaminating the stream. Then all those germs from so many people coughing. A way the virgin has, I suppose, of strengthening your immunity.

Some say Lourdes' holy water consists of the Blessed Virgin's tears alone. Bernadette herself, though, never claimed this, scholars generally concede. The fact that people persist in preferring their Mary weeping is a fact regardless. And if she's so upset—to the point she keeps appearing to young virgins mired in poverty, draping even wraiths of herself in arrant lacrimony, flooding a grotto and instating a site of pilgrimage—I wonder why she doesn't just end it already.

A woman who could do anything could kill herself presumably without access to razor blades. But perhaps this is the only limitation of immortality, life's sheer endless, antic spree, in which you never can sleep for long enough, always waking to another morning with yet more broken people imploring you to heal their bodies. You can never end what demands to keep going. Life remains the tyrant. From eternal life there is no resting.

My mom never realized I could get so tired of this living, and I'm glad I spared her the knowledge, if only because she had enough suffering. For a time, my sister shared some of my same melancholy, only more publicly. My mom drove two hours to where she went to college to ensure a team of doctors pumped her stomach clean. Whereas I only shared with her some of my poetry, making it easier for her to understand why I found it hard to publish.

And in Seville, you find as many gelato stands as you do in Italy, enough to almost make you forget France lies in between. Even in November when we visited, it melts all too quickly.

The atriums of European churches typically house the baptistery, a result of Christians converting Roman mansions into houses of worship, mansions whose water source stood at home's entrance. For later worshippers, this assumed symbolic significance, allowing them to purify themselves with water hallowed by a priest, cleansing themselves spiritually if still staying a little dirty before religious ceremonies. And when I found gelato sticking to my arms I'd bared in the autumn heat, I skipped to the nearest chapel across the street, where the water's minerals mirror those in every other building across the city. Where there is no soap but the water is cool, colorless, soothing.

My husband thought this hilarious, and I agreed—the convenience and serendipity. Although neither of us ever pray to anything, leaving that to people with souls worth saving, we both looked up at the statue of the virgin, garbed in rococo vestures overlaying a body carved from an Italian rock quarry. She smiled beneath layers of velvet while her wrists were ringed in bracelets.

Were I to pray by some miraculous something, it would not be to the Blessed Virgin but to my mom, who had sex, yes, but I'm sure not frequently and not until her early thirties, when she married. Were I to pray to her as if to some god or a saint, I would beg her for her love only. For the healing it once brought me.

And she would look up, with her lower lip quivering, nervous she might say the wrong thing to a daughter who might slit her wrists into a scarlet effluence once she flew back across the Atlantic. Waving to me sheepishly, she would fade into the storm clouds through which the virgin had started peeing. And I would be left there standing, saying nothing to the woman who ignored me. Crying into the baptistery, leaving instead of entering.

As it was, I turned at the door still open to the gelato stand across the street. I walked back inside the chapel and stood again beside the font of holy water no holier than that flowing from any sink. With my hands now clean, I rubbed each arm again. And looking toward the altar, I saw my mom's face recede. The virgin's lips thinned into a smile from which I saw her teeth blacken. Her eyes alone were weeping glass, hard things.

Visions of Animals

"You do not have to be good.

You do not have to walk on your knees

for a hundred miles through the desert, repenting.

You only have to let the soft animal of your body

love what it loves." —*Mary Oliver*

"He imagines a necessary joy in things that must fly to eat." —*Wendell Berry*

Pterodactyls at Flight

As snow fell on the last Saturday of April, Rich dropped the ring I was no longer wearing down four marble stairs. And for this, nine years later, I was grateful, for the voice of something falling that caught the light on its way down, for the tinkling note of alarm after "Pachelbel's Canon" was finished.

We were taking the same flight from Chicago to New York, where he lived and I was going to visit. We were taking the same flight but only by accident. And as I watched my husband's best man disappear onto the jet bridge while I ate a hummus sandwich at line's end, I wondered if he would turn around and recognize someone he forgot existed. I wondered, realizing I had always wanted to be a pretty girl for him, realizing I had not succeeded. Still I wanted him to know I had evolved from a pterodactyl into a woman choking down a crust of bread. I wanted to offer him an explanation.

I'd evolved from predator to prey and was still falling down the food chain, farther every minute. My wings had atrophied into two blunt bone stubs, I wanted to tell him if I could only attract his attention. My legs had shot out from a pelvic bone shaped into a moth for unknown reasons. Both went limp as worms now in the tub, and I'd be nothing but a white worm next, I wanted somehow to warn him. I'd grow twice as long every time someone cut me in half. Only the smallest, whitest worm devours more meat than a girl and pterodactyl combined, masticating everything except the bones from the bodies left behind.

I watched him duck inside the nave of the plane, wanting him to see me clearly. Yet I expected some flying dinosaur to come snatch me by my neck the while, as I did always, because you don't have to be a pretty girl to make a tasty piece of meat.

You have to look a pterodactyl in the face, in other words, to see just how much uglier I could get. Only this is too much to ask of any man with turtle eyes green as any swamp, a man looking down for fresh fish from his rock and never up for vultures. This is too much to ask of any New Yorker eyeing girls perched on stools in every coffee shop, girls who have never eaten a lizard. Girls who have never known the keen frustration of sitting with their seatbelt strapped inside a plane when you once had your own wings without feathers, when the bones of your back still flap midair so you arrive exhausted to your destination.

It had been more than three years since we'd seen each other, he said when he saw me standing halfway down the aisle. This, I said, was only because I'd left three tampons in for two straight weeks when I came to New York last spring. I was sick all trip; I almost died of sepsis. Otherwise, we'd have met a year ago, for pretzels and beer and whatever else turtles in Brooklyn liked in the early evening.

I'd gone to the emergency room two days after my husband saw him in Williamsburg without me, I said, projecting my voice so he could hear me clearly. I shoved my bag in the compartment above my seat and said three tampons left so long inside me had made me start to stink. And I didn't want him to think I reeked as well as looked aggressively unattractive. The fact I was sitting only a seat away from him this moment I thought I owed to eating a daily spinach salad. I was too healthy for three tampons left in too long to kill me, I added. This while he took an eye pillow from his backpack and pulled the shade almost shut, so a slim saber of sunlight struck me from above his elbow crook.

He said this morning had been the end of a weeklong librarian conference, when he'd had too early a meeting. So it was lights out once the plane took off, he told me after repeating his astonishment at seeing me again, here of all places. Got it, I responded, promising not to wake him, feeling far less surprised about the odds myself. The ring missing from the fourth finger of my left hand I saw no reason to mention. I wasn't wearing it because I was having it resized, I kept silent. Because losing weight by degrees almost too small to notice was only a sign of the worm to come.

But I would want to wake him, I knew as soon as I promised I wouldn't, because I don't like letting someone else sleep so long as I'm still conscious. I also thought I maybe looked nicer, in my new and nautical dress, than when he'd seen me three years before. I thought he might want to examine my epaulettes while thinking about turtle flesh, how it tastes to birds of prey spinning them over on their carapace.

He could reflect on turtle flesh until he smelled it, then consider how pterodactyls transmogrify into women. Falling perhaps too slowly unconscious, he could try to comprehend how birds such as this can become only passably pretty girls at best, with their chromosomes still wriggling with the worm to come next. Because some things make sense only at higher altitudes, where a woman once a bird of prey herself still tires from the effort she no longer makes to keep herself aloft.

After closing the shade shut of its last light sword, Rich introduced me to the woman who sat between us, another librarian wearing glasses and a suit the color of an artichoke. I shook her hand knowing I might have simply smiled instead, because I own no suits and eat few artichokes but was wearing a striped and nautical dress with brass buttons at my breasts. Then I leaned across her lap to tell Rich I'd sat beside a man who bought me a bloody Mary the last time I'd flown to New York a few days before my husband, back when I was dying of sepsis without knowing it. When the plane taxied to the gate, we exchanged email addresses. We'd never written a word but gotten a little drunk.

To me, Rich still looked as if he could be my husband's older brother. My husband was only ever his wingman when they were younger. My husband talked to the pretty women, and Rich went back to their apartments. My husband was still such a lost puppy in the wilderness, I said as he pulled his eye pillow down over his forehead. Puppies, though, are sometimes a little too tender of meat for someone who once ate turtles for breakfast. Puppies are not always the best company for pterodactyls who are pterodactyls no more.

With Rich asleep and the plane alighting on the cloud cover, I opened Mary MacLane's *I Await the Devil's Coming*, a memoir of a 19-year-old written in 1902, a memoir so histrionic it was really quite funny, I told him earlier during the safety demonstration. I promised then again I would not wake him, to which he nodded glassily, too trusting. His beard was a studied nine-day shadow against a nose shaped like escargot at its bottom. Mary MacLane, I realized before we reached our cruising height, awaited the devil a good long while, but she never got to know him. She knew the devil as little as others know Jesus, awaiting him with equal avarice. She knew nothing of divinity or its opposite, only of hunger unmet, of lust abstracted. She was a predator without prey as yet. A tiger in a pig pen, as most adolescents are and too many remain to their lives' end.

As Rich lay slumped against the window and began to snore, I read the devil worship of little Mary MacLane, wanting all the while to tell him the only thing I could that could ever matter to a man certain to live all his life devouring one pretty girl after another. To live a more satisfying life, I almost hissed but didn't, you have only to embolden your appetite, to begin slaying larger prey and eating with your fingers. You have to kill for your dinner while letting your chin drip with fresh, red nectar. It's the only explanation there is, I wanted to assure him but never managed, why hungrier creatures commit more carnage. It is why tigers live longer than barn cats, for instance, why this world has become a vast, spinning abattoir where most of us go to bed with half-full stomachs.

Then having been such a pretty pterodactyl with a taste for ugly meat, I wanted him to fatten himself, to feed on worms if there was nothing more savory to fill him. Woman as I was, with nothing but a hummus sandwich still with a little less than half to eat, I knew nothing mattered more than hunger satisfied only to hunger again in only a few more hours. I knew that all reality, in New York and Chicago and the skies in between, derived from the turtle eating the worm so that something else could swallow them both then die and be eaten by more worms to come.

Had Rich not slept the whole flight, had the topic somehow arisen in the course of conversation, I also would have told him that my mom had once sewn me two cotton wings for a dinosaur play when I was six or seven. The pterodactyl's song was the saddest, and at its last refrain I collapsed my wings. I distanced myself from the fans at stage's end, fans that had earlier made them float through wind. I pretended to die at song's finish though my teacher said I needn't. She said I could simply bow and smile instead like the brontosaurus. Still I eddied and withered like leaves in autumn. I stumbled tearfully back to the chorus.

I talked to him in my head, because words, even when unsaid, are what we give each other when beauty has gone missing. With enough of them, we can tell ourselves who we are when we look in the mirror for someone we hope is pretty and see only a woman whose wings have shrunken into bone stumps instead. Someone who eats her spinach but whose stomach still growls with hunger everlasting.

When he opened the window as the flight attendants began to prepare for landing, I squinted at the light reflecting off the wing. Rich pointed toward a brown brick high rise in the Bronx, saying he had lived there in high school. He was adopted as a baby, I knew, and both his adoptive parents were long since buried. I said he had quite the view, overlooking the Hudson. He nodded and said he'd help me find my way to my hotel in the Village where a fireplace was lit in a cool late spring, where the French restaurant attached to the breakfast room served turtle soup. So that I would feel at home, surviving on amphibians as I used to.

If a pterodactyl devours turtles, what does a woman once a pterodactyl herself devour? A woman devours devils, which she expels from her womb roughly every 28 days, when she plugs the hole between her legs with a swath of cotton in the shape of a shrunken phallus. And if she suffers a lapse of memory or is just too long used to perhaps too large a partner, then she does not feel the cotton shaped inside her at all, not one or two or even three, and subsequently nearly dies of trying to stop the bleeding. She misses seeing the best man at her wedding in Brooklyn for a beer or two. She sees him on flight a year later, though, by accident, when she is dressed like a sailor turning into a worm with her wedding ring at the jeweler's being shrunken.

The day before my wedding, I weeded my mom's flower beds and read half *The Brothers Karamazov*. Next morning, I washed my hair in the sink but forgot conditioner, so that my hair tangled in the snow. Rich's girlfriend helped to comb then tried to tease it with a curling iron, but the tease refused to harden. Three weeks later, my husband said Rich slept with her best friend and the relationship ended, when he moved from Chicago to New York to sleep with someone different. Several times now in New York the process has been repeated.

On the bus into Manhattan, I asked about his girlfriend of a year now or two when he told me he'd broken up with her about a month before. She wanted to move to Seattle, he said, for the mountains. Mountains were things best enjoyed from a distance, I responded. The problem with people in Seattle was everyone wanted to climb one, while I preferred grass growing on flatlands. Dandelions were my favorite flower for any odd bouquet you might watch wilting at a wedding reception.

He said when he'd visited Seattle with her the summer before the city had been nice, however. Nicer still the helicopter ride they'd taken over Mount St. Helens a few days afterward. To survey the wreckage, I offered, imagining the blackness below. No, to witness the regrowth, he replied more softly than I'd expected. The wildflowers were endless, he added, while I looked toward the Empire State Building's spire. Each petal a thousand times bluer than the sky.

What do you need beauty like that for when you have this traffic? I joked while the bus stalled on the freeway. Then I laughed loud enough for us both, because I would have liked to see those blue wildflowers more than anything.

At Union Square, he pointed me toward 8th Street, saying I only had two blocks to walk to go. Looking over his shoulder at a woman with hips flared into lotus blossoms, he asked where I would eat this evening. I said I had no idea but would enjoy wherever it was. Because I was waiting for no one, no devil or puppy or divinity, and could eat whatever I chose.

We hugged, I smiled, and he said, What? as I waved goodbye. I didn't say anything, I responded, when he laughed, explaining I looked like I had more to say. I smiled and waved again, repeating how good it was to see him. Then that I was sure he'd find himself another girl to replace the mountain climber, of whom there were far too many in this world as it was.

I said everything I'd needed to except that my teeth were beginning to shift in elevators. They were detaching from their gums while my scalp was molting from its skull and the voice of a woman hidden behind the buttons announced the next floor to come. I assumed the woman had perfect teeth as well as a voice that never weakened. Her skin, I imagined, was pasted to her bones with glue that never came unstuck. Whoever the invisible woman inside the elevator in my apartment complex was, I wanted to tell him but didn't, she might be the one. She spent all her time running from lobby to penthouse and so her legs were strong. But she lived in Chicago, so he would have to move back quick, before she found someone.

I had forgotten to warn him too I might be a worm the next time we saw each other, which I knew wouldn't be too soon if ever. I would be wearing my ring again, a half size smaller than it was before or maybe even smaller, and I would grow back twice as long any time someone chopped me up. All birds were birds of prey to a worm of any length, and so I wouldn't live much longer. I was relieved, though, I wouldn't have any hair for any girlfriend of his to try to curl, hairless as most worms are. Next time I saw him, I wouldn't bother with trying to be pretty and failing. I would do nothing except slither through apples.

Inside my hotel room, a bronze hand wrapped itself around the base of the lamp above the bed. Its fingers were thin as talons, as if nothing but bone gripped a string of fraying filament. Even with the lamp lit, it was still too dark to read my book. I put little Mary MacLane on the windowsill so that she could look out for the devil herself, somewhere in Washington Square Park or somewhere else, and placed my fingers over those of the hand with electrical wires where the marrow should have been. Where all the blood, I'm told, is made, inside our body's whiteness.

And walking to a sushi restaurant within the next few minutes, I saw the devil in the flesh. Because you do not have to wait for these things, Mary. The devil comes to you.

I saw a woman with skin smooth as a mannequin walking toward me. As she came closer, her eyes fixed on my midriff. She stopped me and said that she had always wanted to wear a sailor dress herself but that I looked prettier in it. She had sunglasses on, so I couldn't see the color of her irises. I felt, though, they were red as her fingernail polish.

I thanked the devil then slowed my pace, feeling less hungry than before. And seeing men turn their heads to watch me pass, I felt my pelvis trying to flap its wings, molded in the shape still of a moth for unknown

78

reasons. I felt my bones struggle for movement and ache with exhaustion. I felt the devil's gaze warming my back, where my wings were once but had long since fallen.

I knew the devil recognized a pterodactyl a pterodactyl no more when she saw one, because old birds of prey identify each other by scent alone, the aroma of fresh carrion. And those who feed on dead and dying things know a woman whose skin is loosening from her skull and whose gums detach from her teeth when she rides an elevator. She may look pretty for a moment, inside her new and nautical dress, but the devil knows she'll wriggle the rest of her life inside an apple other pretty women will eat for knowledge of how to satisfy the hunger that never does vanish.

Stray Tigers

Three and a half miles from our home, across a cement bridge straddling a river where children without shoes fished with their hands, stood a house and barn once owned by my dad's younger brother, Nelson, who shot himself in the October brume among his Herefords before I was old enough to miss him. I remember nothing about him except his sideburns, brown caterpillars that clutched his cheeks. Buried in a mahogany box, they became a permanent chrysalis.

The cows stayed above ground, however, where my dad began feeding them in Nelson's stead, calling out their collective name of "calf, calf" from his cloud-colored truck as we trundled down an ochre road. Together, we scooped corn and hay into rusted troughs. We fed them viands sweet smelling enough to tempt me to lick the side of the shovel then rinse my mouth in the cataract of the hose.

Once we were closer to Nelson's home than our own, once we crossed the bridge, my dad inevitably warned me of tigers. He'd nod toward the shoeless children walking the dam's steel skeleton, wrap his voice like a poultice around my ears, and tell me they were prowling the riverbed, searching for laughing little girls to eat. He'd whistle a tuneless reel through gapped front teeth, and I thought how fun, tigers in Indiana.

Decades later, at 29 years old, as hungry as Nelson's cows for my dad's long silenced calf calls and working for a pet magazine in a basement with black mold suffocating the ceiling, I knew for the first time he had told the truth. There were tigers in Indiana, three and a half miles from my home that was no longer my own. They paced the river's silt shallows where shoeless children still fished with their hands. A man with a mythically white beard that told its own time had corralled dozens of white and Bengal tigers into pens made for birthing sows. He pitched them offal from the cows my dad and I fed fat enough for slaughter.

He made a market of the dumpster outside the butcher. He tossed bovine hearts and livers limp as jellyfish through the wire's holes. The fences, the national news reported, were low and feeble. That the tigers would burst them soon was certain. They lunged at potbellied policemen against wire that trembled from their hot javelins of breath alone. Staring out toward the sepia river, they looked as if they would run all the way to Sumatra if they could. These strays against their will.

Only animals, left to themselves, cannot value place the same as we do. They remain at home on this earth wherever they find themselves. To call an animal a stray is to confess how homeless we have become on this planet we are largely friendless toward. It is to confess how homeless we are ourselves.

What we called wild cats, those swallowing mice nearly whole, softened the air above our meadows. They made it mew. I didn't see any reason to enter their lives any more than I did that of the wind. Active nurturing instincts, bound up with warm milk and crying breasts, have never taken root within me. But my sister, possessed of a need to touch, to birth and sheathe from the beginning, trailed their paw tracks across our farmland in a nightgown she pouched into a slack and wrinkled womb. She ferried screeching kittens back inside our kitchen, where she poured them bowls of powdered milk she sweetened with vanilla extract I would have saved for making cookies.

I watched as the cats vacated first the arroyo that became a stream in spring. From there, they fled to a bed of hollyhocks veiled in spider webs then to other, more furtive places. At first, the cats were running but then began to vanish. They were deliberately straying from my sister's palms, and I told my parents she was stealing their oxygen. I said the air was growing harder without them. No one, though, listened. Only now can I see that the summer after Nelson shot a bullet through his ear, the kittens mattered less than they might have done. The hardening of the air was far from the hardest thing. Perhaps if I had roared rather than whispered over the flowering cysts of broccoli and cauliflower I ate each evening, someone might have heard me. But I was very young and no tiger.

Braiding a doll's hair while sitting on our window seat, I watched my sister grasp the weakest of the remaining kittens, which had all drifted to the dark corners of our garden. The cat's eyes, ringed in blood, grew larger the longer she was petted, and at a glance I saw the animal was dying. This piebald breath of clay had languished too many hours in my sister's arms to feed any more from her mother. The oils on my sister's hands would betray her to her species.

The scent alone was enough to mark her as unwild, of being forbidden to stray any further. With a 7-year-old's innate sense of authority, I told my sister to give up the kitten, to return her to her home in the dark corners of our garden. With all the petulance of proprietary love, though, she refused me. A few days before this, my mom had found her clutching a dead rabbit in her sleep, its gray hair falling onto her sheet like dry rain in the twin bed beside me. My sister had found it beneath our swing set and was warming it back to life. When my mom took the rabbit, she was almost finished. It was only cold, not dead, she insisted. She cried all night and kept me from sleeping when my mom took away the carcass.

The cats soon strayed from our farm altogether. Finding a new home became a matter of survival, if home need still come into it, which I think it needn't. A few years later, the remotest contact with cats led my eyes to water, my chest to break out into a blazing butterfly rash. Too long in their presence now and my body forgets to breathe.

I was done with cats, my body had long decided. Still Knopfa, thin with butterscotch fur, arrived in the rain against my lungs' wishes. One drizzly afternoon during my sophomore year of college, my roommate carried her into our kitchen. I told her I was allergic. But in the wake of a recent breakup she needed to make our apartment more of a home, she told me. A cat meant home to her, wherever the cat itself might choose to wander. This she insisted. There was also allergy medication, which I could afford with my waitressing job, she reasoned.

Once I moved out of the dorm the summer before this, my parents brought me my old bed frame, once either Nelson's or my dad's when they were children. Like my sister's beside me, its headboard contained two bookshelves, in which I used to store my stuffed animals and books. Knopfa soon started sleeping inside the left bookshelf, however. Late in the night, she woke me scratching at its base, determined to dig through the wood to her own underworld, I imagined.

When I sat up in bed and stared into her eyes, no one except the two of us and some stray Indiana tigers awake in this world, I knew we were wishing death upon each other. Because she and no one else had seen me swallow two bottles of aspirin over Thanksgiving weekend, when I had decided not to go home but eat carry-out Szechuan chicken. She leapt at me from the radiator when I retched the liquefied chicken and aspirin up together, when I poured myself a soapless bath I slept in. Years before my parents died and our home with it, she alone knew how homeless I already was. She knew there was nothing to do about it except scratch away at old furniture.

Knopfa cared nothing for balls of yarn or squeaky toys that glowed in the dark. She cared even less for the spiraling claw marks she etched into the only relic of home I had near. Wilder than any books I kept stacked inside my headboard, more wanton than Henry Miller or Colette, she flung them all onto the floor with a fillip of her paw.

My roommate and I shared a bedroom, and although our window

had no screen, without air conditioning there was no choice except to open it wide on summer evenings. I wrested its base from a sill matted in dead flies we rarely cleaned. I raised it high enough for endless flocks of birds to fly in and sink their talons into my skin, as my dad always warned they might but never did. When in sleepless exhaustion I finally shoved Knopfa onto the carpet, she walked to the open window and started hopping window ledges of nearby units. She traced the tapering branches of the tulip tree bridging a Montenegrin coffee shop and our apartment building. She sprang and landed on the coffee shop's awning, where I hoped to God she would stay.

For months, I'd convinced my roommate to smoke outside on our balcony. Once it grew cold, however, she started smoking two packs a day inside and keeping the windows closed, using the base of our rotary phone as an ash tray. When I dialed a number, my index finger was blanketed in gray. Within weeks, seeing no better way, I started smoking with her, quitting four months later when she moved back to Minneapolis. For the moment, however, I lay on our coffee-stained couch while she sat with her legs crossed in her underwear on the floor reading a magazine. I surrendered to the pleasure of dragging on my cigarette's slim thigh while staring listlessly up at the tulip tree. I lay there laughing as Knopfa foraged for mice and insects on the coffee shop awning while a fresh bag of cat food sat sealed inside our cupboard.

I wrote inside that coffee shop several nights a week, though only ever to myself. In his native Slavic tongue, the owner freely appraised his female customers' physiques, the language barrier no barrier at all as he replicated shapes he relished in the air with both hands, lingering over well-rounded hips and breasts, then pointing derisively at too pillowy a derriere on its way out the sliding glass door. The first time I walked inside, he traced my outline with a perfunctory forefinger as he stood leaning against the espresso machine while folding a menu into a paper airplane. At the time, I wrote in an almost illegible script since lost to time. What I wrote inside my journals I could not now say. Like Knopfa, I had to wander somewhere, though, even if only across a darkened alley.

Whatever I said so much of to my journals has not lasted, yet the saying of it inside a coffee shop with the paw prints of a cat I wished dead smeared across its awning made my life feel less lonely than it was. This humid room teeming with hunched, hollow-eyed men speaking strange lisping languages and coldly assessing my body's proportions was a living room that bred real living, I told myself. It was a place where I was instantly more alive than across the street, behind the tulip tree branches and above the convenience store where I bought toilet paper and menthol cigarettes both in bulk. I began smoking here too, not because I savored the phantom reach of tobacco down my throat but because I found it a kind of company when I looked up from my journal and saw no eyes meeting my own. For a few seconds, I could fill the space at least inside my lungs. I could exhale languid eddies of smoke, watch them grope the wings of the ceiling fan, and continue my quiet conversation with myself.

For a dollar more than the price of a single cup alone, I ordered a bottomless cup of coffee so I could stay as long as I wanted. Later, I realized even a bottomless cup of coffee empties itself in time.

After I vomited all the aspirin into my toilet and woke up inside my tub, I forced myself to stop loving a dying man, who sat inside the same coffee shop nearly as many nights a week as I did, reading long-dead souls like Schopenhauer and Spinoza from books with broken spines. I sat across from him while curling my back into a question, trying to seem fragile enough that he might want my love. Arnie was twenty-three years old with Crohn's disease and would not live past twenty-seven, he said with the arrogance of copper just beginning to turn to green, a patina too early in the making. And because he was already balding and his skin was the color of peeled potatoes, I believed him and was sorry, because together, I felt, we could have been very sad for a very long time. We could have sat inside that airless coffee shop our whole lives blowing blue smoke onto each other's faces. Together, we could have been almost half alive, knowing slightly more than the rest of the living if not as much as the dead with whom we kept our company. Together, we could be so endlessly tired of life it would be as if a tiger had eaten us already.

Arnie too was allergic to cats, I discovered. When I invited him over one evening after the coffee shop had closed and my roommate was out of town, he slid my shirt off and began sucking my breasts. Soon, though, he started to sneeze and couldn't go on sucking. He turned his head and saw Knopfa coiling her tail around the radiator. She twitched her ears at him and blinked, when he told me he had to leave. It was only a matter of minutes, he said, before he broke into a rash and began hyperventilating.

Once my roommate moved out in the spring, I opened the window late one evening after writing several pages on Hegel and watched Knopfa wander out to the ledge's far end. Seeing her tail recede onto our neighbor's balcony, I closed the window and didn't reopen it for several days. I stopped buying over-the-counter allergy medication, kitty litter, and cigarettes all within the same week. I started making out with my handyman on Tuesday evenings after a class in French philosophy and dyed my hair obsidian. I burnt candles inside my headboard shelves, letting the wax overspread the claw marks. I let myself stray a little, to feel what it was like not to have a home for a time.

Someone else now scares the cats away from my mom's flower beds and kills the kittens with love. Where I live still, in the densest part of a fairly dense city, I find few stray animals. Those there are stalk alleyways, not riverbeds lined with tigers. Most walk on leashes, barking at their own kind. Most aren't allowed a shadow of an opportunity to stray, to become what nature might recognize as herself.

86

A few months ago, lying on a bath towel on a beach in Puerto Rico with the sound of waves filtered by the music of a metal detector rummaging the sands, I saw a stray dog skimming the shoreline. Like all animals on the island we had seen, the dog was homeless, as untethered as a meteor to some specific swath of land. She rounded another group of sun bathers and angled toward me, speeding her pace as she came closer. She licked my toes and wedged her rump against my hip. Eight black teats melted into my stomach, into our shared patch of sand.

I was reading a short story in which a single woman tells her mom she's sleeping with a married man. I was trying to finish it as the dog nestled her body in closer and nudged me half off my towel. The man waving the metal detector like a blind man's hands came and hovered closer, waking the dog from a half-sleep as the machine crowed at some spare change fallen from someone's pockets. As he left and walked toward shore, the dog again closed her eyes and displaced me from the towel altogether. Making a temporary grave of the cool sand, I shut my eyes to the sun breaching the clouds and gave up caring about the affair of the woman in the book. I lay the paperback open across my chest and lifted my arm over the dog's abdomen. Her body collapsed deeper into my side and together we fell asleep, two tigers tired of roaming, to the sad sound of water running away from our feet.

Two Plastic Ponies

The Buddha's Face

The Buddha is balding. Most consider his hair loss irrelevant, because his hair is not important, because they are more concerned with enlightenment than his appearance. Most have yet to notice it thinning to begin with. I always loved, though, when his hair was longer and more lustrous, when it coiled around his crown, resembling a sleeping serpent.

Sometimes I suspect he's losing his hair on purpose, weaning me from dependence on sensory experience. His hair has stopped growing regardless, making his face of less interest, his face I have never seen because he never turns and shows it, because he realizes how susceptible I am to attachment.

Some nights, I convince myself he was disfigured in a car accident. Others, I'm certain this is only a thinning horse's mane I'm looking at with a horse face in front of it. What I see of his back and buttocks looks human. Still between his legs a horse's phallus may hang off him.

Yet the Buddha never meant for me to mistake his two eyes meeting mine for wholeness—two eyes I only ever imagine—because even in the gaze of a man awakened there lurks division. Even in the face of the Buddha there is the skin between the eyebrows known as the glabella. A small space of separation.

All I know of him for certain is he hasn't had a haircut for as long as I've sat silently behind him. For years, he let me daydream about winding his hair around my neck. But he has since decided I'd best commune directly with life's divine substratum, the closest thing you have to God in Buddhism.

Only instead of meeting God when I close my eyes for meditation, I follow a dark comet that quivers through my cornea, quivering because it's on the brink of either orgasm or nervous exhaustion. It's only a floater, only debris dissolving into blindness, yet has become a quiet companion. It shuttles through what seems the expanses of an outer galaxy but is only the inside of my body. Still I let it buzz and fret and worry when it senses another floater might come crashing. I let it quicken its breathing while the Buddha's hair keeps thinning.

None of the statues of the Buddha tell you this is happening. Some show his hair with kinks in it while in others the curls have slackened. For me, though, his hair's appeal was less its curl and more its hidden mass, because he never did unwind it. Still you sensed that if you ever slept beside him once he let it fall to his coccyx, you could lose yourself inside the onyx tresses. You could die of sweet suffocation.

The Preacher's Daughter

Last night, I took a taxi home after having dinner with friends. My driver asked me whether I wanted to hear a song on one of several timeless topics. Instead of love, loss, or drunkenness, I chose sex, hoping for better lyrics. Then as he drove me from one side of Chicago to its opposite, he sang about a preacher's daughter who slept with men she found attractive, something I'm still unsure whether the Buddha is or isn't.

The song's refrain emphasized how naughty she'd been. To me, she sounded only like someone pursuing something the Buddha has persuaded me I'm better disregarding. Reliance on the pleasures of the senses, he's said over and over again to the wall in front of me, produces only misery. I'm miserable anyway, I've nearly responded, knowing he would only tell me to continue meditating, something made more difficult by the dark comet, whose pulsing distracts me.

For years, I thought seeing the Buddha's face would make me feel the same as the preacher's daughter being ravished, that would he only look at me I'd attain nirvana and stop reincarnating. Seeing his hair still growing thick as a boa constrictor bloated with another animal's body alone now would be an ecstasy. For years, that kept me as close as I've come to happy.

The only thing the preacher's daughter did about which I thought worth singing was speak in tongues while climaxing. Although linguists agree glossolalia is only the façade of a language, I believed the cab driver when he said she spoke God's language when she came, when she howled more likely. Because when you throb with desire for another body, your mouth fills with tongues of flames. Your one tongue multiplies into hundreds of others. They heat then pullulate then fan each other's fire.

Flaming tongues hovered over the heads of Jesus' disciples before they spoke in other languages to preach the Gospel. Yet like many who keep mostly quiet, the preacher's daughter knew more than her father preaching from his pulpit. She knew that tongues of fire don't descend exclusively from the heavens. They can also fly from out your mouth once you open it to swallow another person.

Two Plastic Ponies

Earlier this morning, an elderly man tapped a bell on his bicycle as he wheeled past me down an alley. A small cyst stood left of his bald head's center and looked like the translucent horn of a satyr. I watched it grow smaller as he wheeled toward a line of dumpsters when a delivery driver honked and reached out his arm to smack my bottom. Tucking my scarf deeper inside my collar, I walked on to the corner grocery, outside which two plastic ponies stood stationary on a small carousel while an invisible organist played.

Placing my food inside a cupboard an hour or so later, I could still hear the carousel's music. I could still hear the same melody but could not see if the plastic ponies were dancing. I could not see the old man's horn still catching the light, the veins' sapphire filigree. Looking around my apartment, I was briefly blinded.

A few months before this, I sat in Bryant Park watching another carousel rotate on its axis. *La Vie En Rose* sounded from its speakers as I walked toward a sign to read that "carousel" derives from "carosellos," or "little wars," dating from 12th-century Arabian games, when the cavalry tossed each other perfumed balls of clay while riding to test their agility. Yet in time, the warriors abandoned their little wars for those looming larger. At length, the play horses were impaled with brass and kept from carnage. Craftsmen festooned them with saddles hewn from the same block of wood as kept their hooves uncloven. Sinews once tensile with speed had slowed to something looking frozen.

Inside every carousel I have ever seen, clouds are also spinning. Someone has painted them only a few feet above the horses in case the sky is barren. Yet clouds have always begged for me the question of who keeps them from collapsing to the ground in a foggy heap. As many people as there are clouds, I once decided, people too tall and thin to perceive, each with two arms to a cloud apiece. In this way, I became accustomed to loving people I could not see. Otherwise, the Buddha's hair loss would hardly matter to me.

Stone Lilies

Petting stones is common where I come from originally. While horses run wild trampling vegetation, stones rise from dusky earth like small, round mountains. They're not much company. Still I used to stoop and pet them all the same, perhaps because where I come from live no other human beings. no different. I could pet them if I wanted yet have resisted.

I've approached dogs walking past me on occasion. Too often, their tongues lick my legs wet to dripping, whereas stones don't slobber. Stones too retain warmth from the sun through the evening. They soothe without jumping. None here, though, know me, so I keep my hands inside my pockets. I walk to buy more groceries, wondering if they were really stones I pet from the beginning, if they were not stone lilies. Perhaps they were all once living, their arms outstretched the same as mine toward something they have no way of grasping.

Defined by a prior incarnation, stone lilies are former crinoids, a class of echinoderms still extant. Fossilized sea lilies, they are the remnants of a subaquatic species with a digestive system so rudimentary their mouth opens beside their anus. Their arms, like those of sea anemones, appear to wave to a passing octopus while really they are hungry. They extend cilia cloaked in mucus to absorb freely floating algae, because as hunters they are lazy. Their mouths have no lips, while those of the Buddha, I still imagine, are luscious. Their caramel waves crest with saliva like spume from the ocean.

Stone lilies hardly resemble the flowers for which they're named. The stones themselves are delicate, more so than the marine animals of which these are only brittle remains. And living sea lilies are common in aquariums, though I prefer them dead and buried. I prefer lilies of stone to crinoids still breathing, those always excreting so near their mouths. Were I able to give him anything, this would be all I'd have to offer the Buddha to disguise his hair's thinning. A stone lily to distract him from what is missing.

A crinoid undergoing the process of fossilization—a stone flower in the making—too is much the same as a woman dressing for no one too carefully. Both are becoming delicate to the point of easily breaking while trying to be happy.

I have spent too many mornings looking at strange men while walking. Yes, I am married, but this little room where my husband and I sit watching TV is not enough for me, is hardly much company. I buy too many clothes to fit my body too closely. I substitute new dresses for fresh hands to grope me. I shop online late in the evening when I should spend my time awakening like the Buddha from this long dream I am having.

I have dressed more nicely than necessary for someone who never turns to see me. Half horse as he may or may not be, I've suspected the Buddha of shape shifting, of leaving someone else to meditate inside his body while he assumes another one and goes out for coffee. I've suspected it only because I've tried to desire it into being as a dark comet flickers past.

Time and again, I've attempted to encounter the Buddha casually while wearing my best sweater, boots, and jeans. Only because he never turns to face me, I prefer to imagine this is another woman wasting her time dressing for no one who takes notice. It is someone else looking exactly like me who seeks the attention of a man a near divinity. I am only watching.

I watch as she applies needlessly bright lipstick, as she blots it by kissing a piece of toilet paper she has folded. I watch as she squeezes herself inside a cotton dress the dryer has shrunken. She walks down the stairs in her apartment building as another man opens the door to his unit, as he looks up at her and says sweet Jesus. She is not attracted to him. Yet for this unholy exclamation she feels herself open, above her knees and below her abdomen. She feels herself part and moisten, though while she's home she locks the door to her apartment. Still she knows this is what she wanted if she's honest. For someone she doesn't know to harden while she softened.

Those few species of crinoids that have survived at the bottom of the ocean are finless. They go sailing without direction. They are not attached to any sunken rocks or ships like those ancestors that have since succumbed to extinction. Modern crinoids are evidence that aimlessness is a goal of evolution, while stone lilies are the fossils of those no longer in existence, those that once had something to anchor them.

And place a stone lily just above the ear of the Buddha, maybe while he's sleeping, and you can more easily forget that he's balding. You see only the fossilized sea flowers no one bothered to pluck but died subaqueously.

The Buddha's Offspring

A new art installation has placed hundreds of Buddha heads around the city. A circle of them has appeared in a nearby stretch of parkland. The plaster casts have all been cut off at their noses, allowing them to rest without tipping on their chins, allowing the Buddha to better smell the grass where his half head sits. He has no lips or tongue to taste any dandelions with, an absence that makes his waving hair even more apparent.

Buddhist monks and nuns shave their heads to enter the order and begin pursuing transcendence, though there are different ways of going about it. Ascetics in India tear out their hair with their fingers, while others grow it in a tangled clump then cut it with scissors. Most simply apply a razor to keep themselves looking like newborn babies with longer legs than needed.

A married woman, however, cannot easily shave her hair she used to wear long and flowing. Otherwise, her husband either looks for other women or accuses her of suicidal tendencies. She can be only a woman occasionally desired and desiring whose hair begins thinning, who spends a great deal of her spare time in meditation. I'll become an ascetic soon enough, I tell myself, once I've lost everything.

Getting rid of all the clothes inside my closet too is not a problem, if only because I'm having no offspring, because I don't plan on leaving this world anything, this world I've only paddled to in a coracle to begin with. Yet the Buddha's genes may still be in circulation. No one knows whether his one shedding its stalk and evolving. Still there remains the possibility that someone living has his same features, looking more like a horse than ordinary.

The Scent of Battle

Battle brings no end to any conflict. Its exertions only prolong it, intoxicating those embattled with its fragrance. Yet this world allows for only so much wreckage. In time, all war horses turn to plastic. Still stand too far from any carousel to hear its music and again war beckons.

I was watching the Kentucky Derby at a party where I knew only a few friends and was without my husband when a man offered me a slice of cake then a second. He asked my name and said he noticed I wasn't wearing a floral print like every other woman in attendance. Instead, my dress blazed with red lightning bolts he grazed in passing.

Sipping my mint julep, I sat placid as a duck overlooking Lake Michigan while looking up at the TV. Left to themselves, I told him once he sat beside me, the horses might run at the same speed, though never in an ellipse wound so tightly.

He told me he was playing Jason in a new production of Medea and I should come and see it. Only before Medea killed her children by way of punishing Jason for his marriage to another woman, she helped him find the Golden Fleece, I remembered but didn't mention. When he sowed a field with dragon's teeth, Medea warned him the teeth would become men raising arms against him. She said he would have to toss a large stone among them to make them slay each other. Only she, even here, was longing to go to battle, she the real warrior.

I told him that, although Medea was horrid, I never liked either. A better man would have planted the dragon's teeth without consulting an enchantress too susceptible herself to enchantment. I stood to leave the moment the race ended.

He hugged me while my lightning bolts folded into tongues of flames, both of us knowing this was our first and last meeting. Because his hair was thick and wavy yet his lips thin. Because I am done with trying to be happy as the Buddha has taught me, he who sits so still I wonder if he is fossilizing into something that breaks all too easily.

Antlers in Space

We leapt onto the breakwater at the close of a moonless night, and we'd have walked all the way to the lighthouse wrapped with seaweed if John had done as he liked. Only I told him my arms were beginning to pickle with bumps looking like the eggs of insects, that I was shivering, when we both sat down and started kicking our legs in the surf. Because he had no sweater to give me, he rubbed each of my hands between his own before starting to trace the lines of my palms.

I closed my eyes as he followed the seams of my hands' patchwork and I saw them more clearly for seeing by feel alone. The lighthouse too was lightless. For years it had stood derelict, he said, as if he'd been the one to snuff its flame. Yet the city produced enough light from the windows of skyscrapers as it was while no more ships came here to dock. This breakwater was a useless place if use were your concern. Nothing but a bed of rocks for people like us to fuck.

I told him no, because he had almost become a priest last month. I didn't want to be his first, though I may have been his second or third or fourth, I realized afterward. And I didn't want him to be no good, to hesitate too much, as he'd done when he asked me to meet his mom, who spoke with an Irish brogue and tossed peat inside her Chicago stove, before I'd seen his cock. He left messages on my answering machine playing shoegazer riffs on a banjo he built from a cigar box. He loved to rest his eyes, he said, in the depression dividing my upper lip, my Cupid's bow he called it. He had rarely seen one so pretty, he told me over and over again.

The vertical cleft extending from the bottom of the nose to the middle of the upper lip has no apparent use, only vestigial echoes of when we better leveraged our sense of smell to know what we were eating. My philtrum is larger than most, though perhaps larger is not strictly the truth.

Maybe more pronounced, more delineated by shadows stuck within its groove. Or maybe absent any other feature that stands out, it appears untowardly striking on its own, a holding spot for nothing I have ever known. It has become in any case a hiding place, here at the center of my face, hiding all the love dissolved with antlers in space.

Male deer sprout their first set of antlers at roughly one year old. They turn from animals to half-trees poised to battle another arboreal galaxy with antlers of its own. Their antlers grow a quarter inch per day during April, May, and June. By early summer, their texture remains supple as breast tissue begun forking into lightning bolts. At summer's end, however, the deer's testosterone levels surge; their antlers harden into bone. They go to battle and mate beneath an autumn moon. By December, their antlers all fall off onto longer fallen leaves, leaving bloody depressions over which scabs form then start flaking.

After John had fingered all the lines of my palms, he helped me stand up then grabbed my hips and thrust himself against me. I let him ride me like this, with his cock sealed safely in his jeans, my knees knocking against the white rock's chalk, when I laughed louder than perhaps I ought, saying I hoped he enjoyed his time as a rutting buck. As I laughed, I could see—could feel better yet—the anger of his thrust, the bitterness of the buck kept from bucking on. He who might have been rather good, I thought. He whom I only saw again by accident, because we soon broke up.

Few people ever bother to tell you that your philtrum is alluring. Fewer find you attractive solely for this reason. A groove of skin in your nostrils' shadow is not the same as sparkling eyes or a full and luscious mouth. It is a beauty you have to appreciate for yourself. Still a deep philtrum with ridges straight as hockey sticks is better than having one that's asymmetrical or smoothened into a plate you can eat your dinner off. An unsightly smear on what may otherwise be a face worth lusting on.

Yet a blind man palpating your face, memorizing its contours through his fingertips, still might fall in love with you because of it. He with three children almost grown with an ex-wife whose eyes see into the middle distance while wearing no glasses like your own. He who may have paused his finger there, in the smooth and sweeping prelude to your lips, and may have paused other places had you only guided him. He who knows the world by feel and feel alone.

A blind man's finger once rested deeply in my little groove of uselessness and was in no hurry to leave to get other places. Mine, meanwhile, is so much deeper and more useless than the rest, carved eighteen years before I was dry-humped halfway to a lighthouse long unlit. And its groove has only deepened since, worn by love and nothing else. Love that has nowhere to go but back and forth between my nose and mouth.

Because mine is deeper than the average, I can also travel lighter on voyages. I can store my oddments there, between the twin peaks of my upper lip, for which others might buy another suitcase perhaps. My philtrum is more cavernous than you might imagine, because I have loved so much more than I have ever had reason. And I make no demands of it. Everything it holds it may hide for its own purposes. First-aid supplies and some snail shell shards—beauty all too easy to dismiss if you have a surplus—though mostly debris, I confess, which is to say all I have ever bothered with. All that comes from tossing love into the garbage.

For three and a half years not long after college, I read letters and catalogs and occasionally novels aloud for Eddie, long blinded by glaucoma and living with his girlfriend, Carolyn, above a pancake house. When I walked inside his office, I dropped a fistful of change onto the carpet on purpose. Each time, he named the number of coins spilled at his feet and the amount they totaled.

Eddie had never seen Carolyn's face, no more than he had seen my own and this little groove of desuetude above where Cupid strung his bow.

Had he done so, he might have changed his mind about us both. Aside from an extra space between two molars visible only when he opened his mouth to yawn or swallow, his appearance was flawless. He took pains to dress in as bright of colors as were sold, to more closely resemble the sun that could no longer harm his corneas. And he always smelled of musk, from the gland of a Himalayan buck, lured close to the hunter's bullet from the smell of menstrual blood. Yet Carolyn looked a mess, as any woman blind from birth has a prerogative. She was fat from eating so many pancakes too. If she fell out of bed at night, Eddie knew her value.

Most male deer regrow their antlers once a year while females remain relatively bald in comparison. Velvet-clad horns emerge from their skulls soft as cartilage before turning wooden. They scuttle higher and higher among whipped indigo clouds at dusk until they are bone tired of making more blood, until their marrow dries out and they've punctured the firmament enough. Yet after they break insensate off, you cannot tell the difference between fallen antlers and twigs from trees tonsured of their leaves but still held aloft by torso trunks.

Only the antlers of any buck must go to battle first, before they can join the debris I store in the nook beneath my nose. They must grow as long as they can manage until they're as close as they come to stone, until they can pierce the heart or lung of another buck. Until he falls among more antlers scattered amok.

And what's the point of this? None except some sex, for the male with the biggest tree at his head and the lady he wants to fuck. For the fun of growing branches behind his ears that bear no fruit, only decay among the rotting apples no one ever bothered to pluck.

Being bucked from behind is being bucked blind in effect. Sometimes you might as well not know whose phallus is at work. If you are penetrated hard enough, you couldn't care less about the bucker's appearance. This has long been my favorite position, though I have also pretended I've gone blind while mounted on occasion. This is only by way of practice should my retinas burst, because for years I felt sure blindness would be my penance for refusing to see all that I should, the suffering that comes of loving someone else too much or not loving him enough. I felt I should learn to function more by touch, groping my cupboards for jam or peanut butter with my eyes shut.

And I suppose I eventually pretended enough, because my sense of sight began to weaken, until I needed glasses to see far into any distance. Over time, my prescription has only worsened.

Sometimes I prefer not to see as clearly as I do, though, to be honest. Because I still can see the face of a man who recanted of a vow never to have any sex just to be denied it near a darkened lighthouse. In retrospect too, I can say this: that without entering me through either his jeans or my skirt, it was my hardest fuck. And I've since been fucked fairly hard, though never hard enough. Because a real fuck from a buck gone hard enough should launch you into space, I've always thought. It should force you to reach out toward the great dark nothingness with antlers for arms grasping no one.

My philtrum knows its uselessness, I've recently begun suspecting. It is aware it has no claim to beauty for anyone with eyes that work. Still it must continue to collect dust from far-flung galaxies and to accept it, that and all the unused love accreting within it. Because I cannot flee this face no more than this face can flee this body it is stuck upon, which is not to say I do not think of suicide on occasion, that I would not welcome an end to this at once. Only I fear an end is not so easy as swallowing too much aspirin. I might be born again, with a philtrum shifted right or left, at a slant for punishment.

Unlike those belonging to humans, deer's philtrums have retained their function. They act as a riverbed between their mouth and the pad of their noses, conveying moisture through a netting of capillaries, moisture that a llows the animal to better smell its food and detect the doe's fertility. Animals, though, possess more bodily knowledge while our brains have grown too large and heavy. They are better at detecting desire by smell alone.

The philtrum of a dog or deer has a smaller depression than yours and certainly my own. There is less of a gap between the ridges, so the moisture flows from one sense to another more quickly. For them, there is no such thing as storage of the world's detritus inside so small a cavern. Whether humans with smaller gaps than myself, with less of a superfluous depression connecting nose to mouth, smell better than people looking more like me I cannot say for certain. I only know I am not one of them, that my philtrum collects more and more rubble from the world's wreckage. I only know that inside it I also carry spores wafting from other planets with my face looking out onto space rather than inside at my organs.

Eddie never touched my face, no matter what I imagined. At times, though, I wanted him to, when I felt overlooked by those with eyes that saw as clearly as my own. I wanted him to feel the philtrum replete with debris I suspected of pulchritude and tell me what it totaled. In place of this, he listened to me speak. He said I had the voice of a baby, a baby gurgling with sweetness. He said other blind people for whom I recorded books wondered how young I was, whether I had graduated high school even. Eddie knew my real age and insisted I was an ingénue, that no one with a voice so soft could have much experience.

I didn't want to argue and asked him to trace the lines of my palms. He told me he wasn't a fortune teller, and I said I wasn't either. He felt the lines, however, and counted their number, and I told him this was evidence that I was born with too many to mean I didn't live like a woman my age on occasion, walking a breakwater to a lighthouse wrapped with seaweed.

This wasn't true, however—I knew as soon as I said it—when he only replied I had the softest fingertips. Too soft to have really lived, we both understood was the implication. I hadn't taken off my skirt at the breakwater a couple years ago, though now I thought I might have.

However wildly they effloresce, trees are antlers atop bodiless heads spinning in space. They are vascular defenses poised to stab enemies lurking on other planets as lightless as our own. I am surprised then I have not grown antlers myself, woman as I am, with a philtrum retained only for appearances. Because what is wood except dead, dendritic bone, and haven't I plenty? I have more than enough living matter deprived of blood and so hardly living. And what is a woman with her arms outstretched but a tree writhing wildly in the wind? Life becoming lifeless, the more she stares into the sun, begging for blindness.

And I cannot be the only one. I cannot be the only woman who stores too much of the world's dust deep beneath her nose's bridge and above her lips. I cannot be the only one who feels antlers might be useful to her as well as to any buck.

A friend recently gave me a plastic bonsai tree I need never trim, a ring holder for all intents and purposes. Trees such as these never bother growing, sitting stationary upon a dresser, indifferent to the value of the rings they hold without their arms growing any heavier. Though to a ring resting on a finger or a plastic branch there is not much difference. Both reach toward a sky that refuses to lower itself and come any closer. Though where does the sky begin if not at your fingers' end? Antlers are only hands without sensation, trying to wrestle another buck to the dirt and pull some fingers off him.

Eddie once confided he could smell when I was on my period. I told him I tried to conceal the odor as best I could, with perfume at my wrists. But he said he had two girls of his own, and this was how he knew they were becoming women beneath his nose. He smelled as well as he heard, he reminded me again, while I dropped some change from my pockets to redirect his senses.

I did not want to become the woman I have become, I as good as confessed to him, by way of apology for the odor between my legs wafting across his office. I had decided it earlier, when I was much younger, with my voice almost the same as it still sounded to him. I saw no need to change when adolescence started. I wanted to protect my innocence, under no near threat except my body's growing reception to sex. I didn't want to bleed out my eggs with the moon but keep all of them.

And this was possible, I almost convinced myself back then. It was possible for me with my hands so soft, though they've since somewhat hardened. With some flowering of cysts, my fourth-grade biology teacher conceded as weakly as she could manage, a woman could shed no eggs or uterine cushion that had failed to form to begin with. She would be an abnormality, however. She would be infertile always, a child of a grown woman, whatever she appeared to the contrary. Well that was lovely, I responded. That abnormality would be me, perfectly happy.

Eddie only laughed, saying this was natural. Whether he meant the wish to remain a child or the woman I had nevertheless become I could not determine.

The best bait for any rutting buck is a used tampon if you ask any man with a gun wanting to display a pair of antlers above his mantle. Nothing is more attractive to a deer whose branches have exchanged all their velvet for wood than the odor of a woman's menstruation, the sign she is still fertile.

Why did humans let their sense of smell grow dry as antlers ready to collapse onto the forest floor again? Why did we let it atrophy, the ability to know our world and those who might love us through scent alone? No one can say for certain, though some have blamed the eyes. They theorize that when we rely so much on a certain sense, the others disintegrate in proportion. And this might and might not be accurate, though I would not become blind to test the hypothesis. Now that I'm a woman and there's no reversing the process, I like to see the face of the person I've decided to fuck, even if he only ever mounts me from behind.

Human females are the only mammals to mate when not in heat. Many mammals, including female deer, bleed while remaining attracted to antlers with the farthest reach so long as sex is still in season. Fertility coincides with a purge of blood from their sexual organs, so there is occasionally some messiness while they reach orgasm.

And what of this? Whatever the amount of blood stuck to the buck's penis, there is also, let's assume for argument, very little love for such a small cleft between their lips and noses, for such a fine-tuned organism. The matter remains pragmatic, because there is little use for uselessness when you live deep within the forest. There is little call to evolve beyond your olfactory sense as your primary sexual one, which tells the bucks when the female deer will have them, usually a month after their own antlers have become a permanent erection. Their philtrums becoming irrelevant is not an option.

Biology, put another way, acts as a determinant, so the species can continue on. Sex is not just for fun, to test the breakwater's puissance. Only I am having no children. I am not trying to impart any wisdom from all I've witnessed, from staring with my glasses out onto far-flung stars, an ingénue no more with my voice losing its sweetness. I am giving you neither knowledge nor wisdom nor offspring, you future humans. I am evolved superfluity, with a philtrum needlessly large.

What does a woman have if she doesn't have antlers of her own, only fingertips softer than serve any purpose and a philtrum collecting more cosmic dust with each passing hour? She has these two hands to stretch high into the air, as high and higher as she likes. She has ten fingers to wriggle when she pleases. She has just enough to know she is alive.

The only place for a woman such as this, I know while inhabiting her from her inside, is a lighthouse with its light burnt out, as close to an antler breaching outer space as I can likely come. A place of pure obsolescence to match my face's finest feature. I have still never climbed a spiral staircase inside a lighthouse with an unlit lantern.

I will likely never light it either, because I am always burning my fingertips, the closest to antlers' ends that I can access, when I use a lighter or matches. I light my skin instead of the candle wick, skin that grows dry with winter's encroachment. And instead of approaching breakwater's end, I walk only to the same makeup counter and back, buying lipstick too bright a pink, buying always two tubes at once, so my lips look stained from raw deer meat.

Because in the absence of antlers, children, career, and even very much love, I have these two pink swords at a minimum. With them, I could scrawl some poetry on the walls of a lighthouse if I wanted. If I ever met with another lightless one.

At my wedding reception, I sat beside Carolyn and Eddie. Carolyn, sitting closest to me and wearing a peach suit, stabbed with her fork at her tarragon chicken while I turned to talk to another guest and she dropped it down her lap. A woman old enough to be my mother and with a mouth wide enough to swallow the chicken whole if she wanted couldn't feed herself in public. Green snot soiled her blouse as she started crying. Eddie, sensing more than the rest of us, could do no more than pat her shoulder pad while she wept into her cleavage. To comfort her, he reached higher for her face than he meant to, smoothing her hair instead of cupping her chin still dripping with sauce from the chicken.

Look at a pair of transparent lungs, on an anatomically correct doll or an x-ray either one, and what do you see, honestly? Bronchi spread like branches, I'm well aware, because I've seen the same thing. Because everything reaches, even when it cannot pierce the skin and see outside the body. Even armless things spread their fingers as wide as they can, to reach they know not what, never touching. So if you see me standing splay-legged on a sidewalk extending my arms as high up as I can reach them, don't ask me what I'm doing. I have no purpose here aside from hardening into antlers soon to fall off me.

Bucks kept artificially subject to twelve consecutive hours of light then darkness, scientists have demonstrated, cannot shed old antlers and grow any new ones. Too much regularity—sun deprived of the ability to wax and wane like the moon whose light is only a reflection—and old antlers rot without bothering to fall off and leave their blood spots. Such a world, with too little variation, grows fast short on debris, making a philtrum already pointless of even less service. Too much regularity prevents a philtrum from collecting anything that might serve you on travels outside the country, discarded shards of love you still might find pleasing.

John wanted to take me home to Ireland to visit some of his extended family. Of all the places I've since traveled then, I have avoided the Emerald Isle, with grass so green it's fit to blinding. After my honeymoon to Tuscany, I planned to call Eddie and thank him and Carolyn, though they missed the bulk of the reception. Because Carolyn had to go to her room after dropping the chicken.

Eddie accepted a new job before I left for Florence. Returned to Chicago, I delayed contacting him. Two weeks later, I learned my mom had terminal cancer and no more than a year left to live. I wanted to cry into Eddie's arms, guiding his hands to feel my face and my cleft hiding at its median, storing who knows how much unused love, grown yet more gratuitous in the interim. I had forfeited all the comfort he might give me, though, by failing to call him before we left for Italy, to ensure he and Carolyn had arrived safely home.

After my mom died and my dad soon after, I saw Carolyn sitting behind my bus driver in one of the seats reserved for handicapped passengers. I didn't answer a call from my husband so my voice wouldn't register with a woman whose hearing was also more acute than average. Instead, I sat watchfully a few seats away, following every twitch of her unseeing eyes for any trace of recognition. I got off two stops early.

Why did our philtrums waste away again, aborting their sense of smell so they're little more than a reminder we once may have had better fucks than we're having at present? Because our sense of sight became too vivid, because we looked and looked, greedy for more faces. Because not all senses can operate fully at once. Because for every heightened sense you gain, you lose another one.

Underwater Bees

I have tried to sell myself at so many yard sales but have yet to be bought. I also have no yard, so I'm hardly my own to hock, while my lungs have begun flapping like wings, have become restless things. Only they are vital, and they are leaving. Soon I will have very little to sell even if anyone will buy me.

Browsing my neighbors' yard sales, I unfold the arms of cardigans then stroke ironing boards' bellies. I palpate all things left lying in a patch of grass either front or back of a house filled with rooms from which more lungs deplete the supply of oxygen. Using a nail file left beside ceramic dolls looking glazed in vernix, I shave off parings from my skin. I shave and shed my epidermis into salad bowls crusted with flies finished flying.

Because I cannot sell, I give myself away like this to those wanting more space for their lettuce. I shed my outermost layer on some folding table —skin that otherwise would flake freely off in the bath, so better on a table with a veneer of dark maple—so that I am closer to touching my organs the moment I undress. So that beneath the bathwater there is less of me to scrub for Monday morning at the office, so that when I walk inside with my coffee I am already less of a person. Because I see very little reason to sell your wares if not to come closer to your vital organs, even less not to welcome the bees buzzing at your doorstep. So very few are left.

The house without a yard and made of wood instead of brick was built in 1869, I'd read in a pamphlet. Its first selling point was its age, then, because I like old things that may be dying if not already dead. It was also green with maroon trim, and that was its second, because the colors were of dried blood overlaying a lawn mowed of dandelions. It sat prim and petulant on the eastern border of the historic preservation district that had charmed my mom to pieces we could not put back together again. So we bought it, or the bank bought it, and my mom cosigned the loan on her cancer bed, where she lay all but unconscious from infusion of endless vials of morphine enlarging the veins in her neck into ropes of azure larvae.

The bees guarding our porch hovered flush with the sidewalk, though we never found their hive or source of nectar, though our house sat within a floodwater zone, which raised our rate of insurance. There was the threat of so much water for very few plants among so much cement to suckle such insects. And flooded though the agent told us we might be at any moment, we never saw so much as a puddle from which some birds might make a tub to bathe in. Still we may have been living underwater all along, something I considered only after we moved on.

Some say the bees are disappearing, but where to? I wonder. I have asked myself time and time again and have decided where the world is quieter. The bees have left us for waters too deep for mammals to breathe in, mammals whose lungs hold them prisoner. Lungs that begin gasping once they fill with salt water.

Everyone else's lungs seem to do the same as mine, with little variation. They void and clot themselves with air that thickens with the threat of storms announced by thunder. Yet no one sees that their lungs might want a rest, busy breathing as they are. No one except an old man whose skin looks wizened past all ironing and ought to sell his board. A man who moved from France to Chicago some fifty years before, the only man in all the world who knows that if you hold a parasol at the right angle, fire will shoot from your fingertips, you are very certain. A man who once sold one in a yard now no more his than my mom's lungs are hers.

I know his face, though mine he has little way of recognizing. His I have seen in newspapers only this last December, when his 37-year-old son died of lung cancer without having ever smoked a cigarette, it was reported.

His lungs were thin as moth or butterfly wings—there's not much difference between species besides their antennae's silhouette—only no one knew this until their dust coated the doctor's fingers obsidian.

The week after his son's funeral, he decided to return to France and close his creperie, which he himself had painted lilac and faces an independent movie theater I visit fairly often.

I know too that he has changed his mind in fact. He has decided to stay in Chicago rather than relocate to Paris. A friend offered to become his partner in place of the son with lungs that charred themselves on the creperie's table lamps. Lamps with their filaments always croaking at a flicker, lamps the old man sold and rebought at a flea market. And I know he cannot remember me no matter how many times I have walked inside, because when a movie lets out his little room grows crowded.

Still I know he would buy me and my two little lungs regardless, could I only offer myself for sale on someone else's patch of grass. I know because only a broken-hearted man like this would want a woman who shaves her skin into used salad bowls available for purchase and uncrosses the arms of cardigans. A woman who bought herself her only parasol in Paris.

Three weeks after our wedding, my dad called to say that cancer had eaten holes in my mom's bones and that her lungs were beginning to flop and make abortive flight patterns. I dropped the phone, folded myself over our futon like an old sweater tossed inside a hamper, whispering, Not Mommy, anyone but Mommy, hammering my fists into my husband's sternum with his jelly heart behind it, telling him I wished he were the one dying. Anyone but Mommy, I repeated. She who had once made our yard much too pretty to clutter with any socks and sweaters better made into pot holders.

Yet Mommy was dying in spite of what I wanted, and we left Chicago for the little green house guarded by bees we fed no flowers. Within a few months, we both got the jobs we told the loan officer we had already while still living in Chicago, while still trying to secure the credit to buy a house so small we had to hunch to fit inside its entrance.

A dollhouse come to life, with molded gingerbread framing its front porch swing, it should have cost doll's money also. We still thought flood insurance hilarious in a place so far from any coast, though this meant eating out was not an option. A clawfoot bathtub sat ursine and indifferent to all our afflictions beside a toilet atop tile the color of moss. No door separated the upstairs bathroom from the study adjacent, so one of us often sat on the pot shouting to the other below in the kitchen, requesting our potatoes mashed instead of boiled with meat we ate tepid.

In the corner of the study, beneath a slanted roof, we placed the threadbare armchair my dad gave me after warming it with years of flatulence. I sat there evenings and read or talked on the phone to Mommy while above my head I heard a rhythmic scratching—the claws of bats, we later learned without wanting to know.

I have too many and too few things and the same amount of vital organs as anyone else. I have one heart and two lungs that empty then refill themselves more times than I'll ever count, organs that are almost too alive to bear, so close beneath my skin. My lungs divide me from the moths and butterflies and bees, which have no lungs themselves, only holes at their thorax connected to their trachea and known as spiracles. They have only a pair of gossamer wings to flap in place of lungs with lonely dreams of becoming gills.

Yet while they're still with me, I would like to lie my lungs in the cool green grass, just to give them room, to let them inflate and deflate themselves without a windpipe always coming between the two. So that I can breathe like a bee through the pores in my skin while awaiting the bidding for the rest of my body. So I can dive light and lungless beneath the waves and become the world's first underwater bee-woman. So I can lay my eggs in the sand and hatch a colony, where the world is always quiet and where the world began.

Yet once I give them a wide enough berth, beneath a table littered with socks and dolls here at the lawn at my feet, I fear my lungs would take advantage. They'd likely no longer be contented with watching the butterflies among the dandelions. They would do more than simply breathe for a change, I'm guessing. They might start squawking, trying to flip themselves over, just to tan the other side and even out their color. They'd take to mocking their own kind more than likely, those lungs still billeted in some flesh, gasping for air among the ironing boards with no legs to stand upon and walk any farther in the distance.

They would easily embarrass those organs still hyperventilating inside some young woman after her mother has left her orphaned. I think as good as know these lungs growing only rowdier by the hour would start shouting, Where to? Where to? Where to now? as if they had anywhere to go once their oxygen supply ran out. As if they could up and walk away from the body they'd abandoned, the body with all the feet. The one still standing and filing her fingertips into salad bowls.

Next week, I'm going to dance with my parasol on stage, spinning it like a wheel fleeing downhill for a performance with my troupe, to circus music composed for the can-can dancers of the Moulin Rouge. Because dancing with a white-fringed parasol you bought in Paris' Left Bank is what you do in Chicago when your lungs hang still captive within their rib cage, when they flutter faster the moment you approach a body of water. They have little more to do to entertain themselves after you've offloaded all the bowls and lamps from your little green dollhouse and moved back into an apartment, where you eat once more as often as you please across from a theater whose independent movies make you no freer.

Bees breach the water no more than butterflies or moths. They have yet to learn to paddle their feet, while our own lungs will sustain only so much weight from the ocean. Our lungs will breathe only through a tube tied to a boat for oxygen and even then for only so long a time. Which is my way of saying that bees that can breed underwater, with something close to gills while still erecting their honeycombs, remain possible if undiscovered, a far-flung relative of the bees we know. Could we only sink to the ocean floor without our lungs collapsing, we might be stung by them among the whales' warbles, meaning lungs lain on some lawn may also breathe on their own. Moths and butterflies both morph from worms into winged creatures, so stranger things have happened already. Stranger things still may transpire beneath the ocean. If I spin my Parisian parasol fast enough for the moment, its edges blur into a plume of smoke with no flames at its center.

My parents both told us not to buy the house, something so small for such a large amount. Released from the hospital and on a lower morphine dosage, my mom expressed astonishment she had consented to cosign the loan, knowing we had no jobs when we opted for a mortgage, knowing we were sure to quit the ones we'd gotten once they became boring.

For her last birthday, I took the afternoon off work so I could watch her disappear. In the past three months, she had lost half her weight and all her hair. She stood four inches shorter than she had only a few months ago and had to roll her pant legs up not to trip on fallen honeycombs. She alone was tiny enough to fit inside our dollhouse without getting a cramp from squatting beneath a ceiling lowered like clouds from which rain would soon begin to fall. She alone was small enough not to grow restless within its walls, which the bats had already begun to topple.

While the bees gargled outside the door with salt for their sore throats, we ate two slices of the lemon cake I had baked the night before. I sang her happy birthday and we cried through the tines of our forks, although we might have cried even if one of us was not becoming a ghost. Because we were good criers, she and I, maybe the best ever born gasping. Maybe this is the reason still why no one will buy me in any yard. Because I am drowning all the bees with water of my own making.

Licking her fork with a tongue whitened from chemo, she told me my teeth needed cleaning, honey dumpling. She said that two cups of coffee a day had begun to leave a film and the time had come to give them a burnish. Perhaps I was decaying too, I said, so I might not have to live long without her. She had her own teeth cleaned only last week and spread her lips to show me the difference. Yet the icing on the cake was yellow, and I saw only the same jaundiced archipelago of extra enamel as had covered her right front tooth before. I also couldn't help wondering why she bothered when cadavers keep their mouths closed.

Still I had my teeth cleaned soon afterward, when the dentist found eight cavities. I drove back twice to the office to have her fill them with a metal amalgam then owed a thousand dollars, which brought my bank account balance to little more than a hundred. In the middle of December, our heater broke, and we put two thousand on a credit card. A month later, we received a letter stating our property taxes would climb nineteen percent by next April. Our little dollhouse, flanked by underwater bees, we could no longer afford, though I had just bought an antique Singer sewing machine and vintage hat stand with more credit. All soon to be sold again at a yard sale without a yard.

My husband harangued me from the toilet amid its moss tiling. Why couldn't we have rented an apartment? he asked, the more loudly when I stayed silent. In this same neighborhood if we had wanted, in some place less cramped and less petulant? We now also needed termite protection, priced at fifteen-hundred dollars more. The whole decrepit house was wooden and would fall down on top of us while we slept. Endless white worms were eating the siding each day more. A hunger that left only holes behind it.

Then my mom died as expected. She died, and we sold the house to a couple with hair both a little too blonde to trust but meeting the bank's requirements. We hired a realtor who liked other men to bite his nipples, he told us by mistake via text message, who made chocolate chip cookies for our weekend open houses and blew up balloons looking like condoms then tied them to our mailbox. We sold our little green dollhouse for the same amount we bought it for and paid a seven-percent commission. Only because my mom had taken out a loan with a twenty-percent down payment, we received a check just big enough to take us to Europe for a month while we languished in debt and didn't speak the language. Two weeks after moving back to Chicago, we left for Paris, where I bought a $100 parasol fringed in white that only made my teeth look a little yellow in comparison.

Somewhere between Chicago and Paris, I acquired a new smell. It was redolent of rotting eggs, said my husband, as if he had eaten some himself. Because I was decomposing, I explained to him. Because a parasol, even one pretty as this, heals nothing. Because when you spin it, it only becomes a wheel that escapes downhill, forcing you to chase it.

In the yard sale we held on a slim stretch of cement a week before we moved, I sold most of my mom's clothes, those she thought that I might want though I didn't. Her sweaters I sold to a teenage girl with a plastic butterfly holding all her hair above her neck. Yet two pairs of her pants I kept and made into shorts too short. I had my mom's legs still if nothing else. Best not to hide them, she said as much herself.

In the dance routine we are to perform within a week now, only one woman has a parasol as a prop. Another must pretend to spin a plastic plate with a hole at its center glued atop a stick, fooling the audience. A third dances with a top hat and does a cartwheel, while a fourth twirls batons tied with ribbons. Originally I was assigned to the spinning plate. I attempted to balance the stick on my palm while using my hips to keep the rhythm. Our first day of practice, I told everyone I had my own parasol at home, that I could spin it fast as a tire rolling down an escarpment too steep for a car to follow it. Then another woman in our troupe, with iron hair and knuckles in her cheeks looking like they could do some damage, grabbed the parasol without asking. She left me with the plate that splinters from the center where the hole is only growing larger.

Last week, the woman broke her toe while trying to twirl the parasol, however. A parasol that was not her own, I'll add, that does not make fire shoot from her fingers, as do those bought in Paris. I watched the one toe break without reason while her other toes bent their same direction. The only explanation was that she was stung by bees buzzing underwater. Meaning she and I are both dancing—she with the parasol first and now my turn—beneath waves that will crush us in time and not soon enough, I have a feeling. Meaning so many years after my mom's death and I have yet to breach water's surface. To let my lungs exhale in the stare of the sun.

I have asked her, for so many years now, Are you happy, Mommy? Yes, I'm happy dear, but only because I have no body, she responds the same each time, until I'm tired of hearing.

No bones to be eaten into holes, no lungs to flutter to a flop, and no more teeth to clean, she cheers. Then she assumes her old body for yet older times' sake and unpeels her lips from her gums, revealing two white rows of evenly spaced teeth, the right front absent its archipelago of yellow enamel so there's now no place to land upon. Instead, there are only glacial waters to swim in until your arms fall off, back and forth and back and forth again, from one shoal of puce-pink gums to the other one. With no rest in between them.

She tells me the little green house has since fallen. The new owners a little too blonde to comprehend any darkness could not afford termite protection. She says that the little white worms have eaten the little green house away altogether, cleaning it of crumbs. Then she adds that worms such as this, devouring the bodies of houses and people alike, are life's greatest gift.

If I am a very good girl the rest of my days, she cautions, I might become a termite when I am born again, with almost as small a body as I could hope to have, eating other bodies away.

I interrupt her, though, always to ask, So are you a worm then, Mommy? When she replies, ever patiently, I told you I was happy, correct? Because I had no body. And every time someone cuts a worm in two, it only grows twice as long back. So—in case you haven't noticed yet—our world is one that feasts on offal, the vital organs that are not so vital once you're dead, sweetie.

I tell her I understand yet am not terribly happy about it. That is only because you still have a body with lungs inside it, she interposes, with a whistle through teeth that are not there any longer, the one still jaundiced, I hope in her sarcophagus. Then I think of telling her I am soon to dance with a parasol, that I feel flames piercing my fingertips when I practice. Soon, though, I think better of it, watch her smile recede into the scythe of the moon that reaps no harvest.

I finish eating my crepe, letting her continue. Seeing I am no longer inclined to talk, she taps me on the shoulder with her bodyless body now and says, No hurry to shed your skin husk before its time, dear. You've still got my legs, however scarred your knees from so many fallen bike rides.

When I say, scarcely audibly, whispering only to myself and sure that she has gone, that yes, she has given me legs just nice enough to attract the attention of a man whose son has left him. A man who will not return to France after all. A man who is the only person who might buy me in a yard sale should I ever find a yard in which to offer my still breathing cadaver. He with lungs turning back to gills like my own, lungs thinking they are flying while they dissolve into something better made for underwater.

If someone buys me, though, before my teeth litter the tub after detaching from their gums, I can spin my parasol before another woman's broken toe becomes unbroken. My lungs can empty and refill themselves, a thousand times in an hour, for something more than air alone. For something close to love. For love from a stranger a stranger no longer. For the taste of honey hanging from a hive long barren.

Painted Metal Bird

Whirling dervishes do not whirl. They spin slowly as spores, in no hurry to reproduce into another unflowering fern sprouting yet more sex cysts along its spine. Carried from one mosaic tile to the next by no wind and no breath, they rotate like languid ballerinas atop a music box whose melody is beginning to unravel into the strum of fingernails on a broken pane of glass. Their conical hats look overtall, their faces needlessly smooth and nacreous, with sprigs of beards just dark enough to remind you these are men beneath their billowing skirts. The play of the lute behind them gradually extinguishes the body of desire, a body turned more than turning. Their palms are thrust up like platters, weighted with only apples of air.

Like the planet itself, whirling dervishes have nothing in particular to do, nothing beyond rotating around an axis. Yet they are wise enough to spiral slowly so as not to grow dizzy. And this, as everyone who has ever spun on an island of sparse green grass knows, is not easy to do. Sooner or later you fall on your head, where your body is hardest but also houses the most holes. You escape within your own small wind tunnel for a time. Your vision blurs and you no longer see the line where sky meets land, yet that is all. Your head hurts for nothing.

Dervishes are seekers, not runaways, however. They twist themselves slowly as any reasonably round, blue-eyed planet while pursuing the divine. For my part, I don't much care who spins the spheres or why. My only concern is this longing that causes me to spin myself so I no longer see those silhouettes walking shoals sinuous as alligator tails on the window's other side.

Earlier that afternoon, my husband had bought me an evil eye tied to a silk rope so short I could see the pendant only through a mirror the salesman held to my neck. Wearing it now, I still have to feel for its pupil, raised into a nipple I know is black and lightless, because I have never bought a longer rope. I joked with two Australian brothers taking our same three-day tour that this was my way of telling friends back home I'd been to Turkey, though few would notice, those few who did wouldn't ask where I had gotten my necklace, and beyond that I liked the idea of an eye that never blinked.

Turks, to their credit, believe in evil, only the kind you can stare down with a hard enough gaze. Yet before there is evil, there is pain. And before pain, sometimes there are letters filling splintered shoe boxes lining the back of your bedroom closet, written to no one with any face to put a name. You wrote them while wearing a nightgown falling to your feet, when you loved no one of identifiable form or feature, as the dervish loves the divine. You wrote them at a time when love alone was enough to assure you there was a divine to begin with, because one person or two or even three would never absorb all the longing that traveled like light beyond any face irradiated in an otherwise empty corridor. They are letters to no one and never sent, your attempt to keep from careening outside your orbit.

Passing each other as if by chance around the sun, planets exchange their share of sidelong glances. This you see clearly after you've fallen to the ground from another spin, because it is so hard to be a world unto yourself, forever traveling your own lone circuit, forbidden all collision. Something unsatisfying in the wholeness of heavenly bodies. Something strange in the estrangement from all touch.

Most planets travel the galaxy pulsing with light they feel burning at their navels yet can never witness. They spin slowly while waiting for stray asteroids' abrasion, looking on at evil from too far a distance. Because whatever carnage it wreaks, evil smells of air after a storm. It leaves life less humid while you ache for further flaying from branches bent by wind. The ache outlasting the fleeting violence acquires its own sweetness. The scar becomes the only consolation for no further scarring. Yet better an unhealed wound than skin always smooth as an olive.

Running water over my hands in the restroom outside the mosque after the dervishes had finished dancing, I looked at the eyelids of the woman beside me in the mirror, eyelids once smoothened by fire, I felt certain, eyelids that coruscated more than the soap that had since run out of the dispenser. Turning off the faucet, she shook her head, saying there was never any soap in holy places. I looked into her eyes, misshapen into oblong pools of black honey, and agreed. God cared nothing for good hygiene.

I said I had some lotion in my purse, however, and held the tube high above her hands, letting it fall like viscous rain. The fire had burnt all the lines off her palms as well as ironed the skin encircling her eyelashes, and I wondered, for the first time, if you could have too much touch. I wondered if I might long for no more stray asteroids myself then. As it was, I left and stood briefly facing the dervish with whom I wanted to spin into a hot, dark wind. I realized that until my own fire came, I'd keep waiting for a crashing.

A sophomore in college, I met Tom on the train while traveling back to my apartment from the Greek diner where I worked nights as a waitress. He was tall and 28, with brown-green eyes that stared off in two slightly different directions, the left looking always just beyond me and above my shoulder while his right rarely left my lips when I spoke to him. He had a girlfriend named Paula I never met living in a nearby suburb and seven siblings he rarely took time to visit.

As an undergrad, he had majored in philosophy and was now in medical school where I was reading literature and beginning to smoke cigarettes in bed. He was rereading Kafka when I met him and told me he fantasized about committing suicide by asphyxiating himself with books on a near nightly basis. Although we talked on the phone more than we saw each other in person, occasionally we met in the dining hall or for coffee, when he would smile, look down toward my chin, and tell me he had never seen such pretty lips. My top lip is too thin, but he only ever saw my mouth with one eye clearly.

One early autumn evening, he began walking me back to my apartment when I invited him in and made us omelets. We ate them on plates we balanced on our knees sitting on the couch I'd found in the alley. After scraping the uncooked albumen into the sink, I sat back down beside him. He pressed his hands into my lower back and said it needed massaging.

A few months earlier, my roommate had painted our living room walls a matte mustard with maroon trim. Casting one eye over our north wall and another over our east while I lay prone across the couch, Tom asked why we had painted the room the colors of McDonald's. I shrugged and laughed, asking him to ply his hands more deeply into my shoulder blades. A few minutes later, he asked again. Still lying with my shirt dangling from the lampshade and my back relaxed into a lazy river, I mumbled I'd had little choice. My roommate was an autocrat, I told him, when he suggested we use the leftover maroon to paint smiling arches across the sliding closet doors, long since fallen off their hinges.

I opened the paint can with a screwdriver and watched Tom paint twin parabolas across both doors while letting streams of maroon drip like blood flowing from a fresh laceration onto the carpet. As I blotted the fallen paint with a washcloth, he unhooked my bra. He shoved me against the refrigerator and painted my nipples the same color as the arches before washing me clean in the shower. The paint, I later noticed, stained the porcelain a pink penumbra.

Later that evening, my roommate switched on the living room light as I was sleeping in the next room over. She woke me and demanded that I buy another can of mustard to cover over the arches before the weekend. But no matter how many coats I applied next day and the day after, their ghost refused to vanish. Tom then left my life entirely, nearly killing himself each night without me.

As I read late into the evening, staring up into the sea anemone limbs of the tree outside the window, his arches reappeared, straddling their legs too widely to resemble any corporate logo. If we saw each other on campus, one or the other of us changed direction. The easiest thing in the world, a dervish knows as well as anyone less holy, is not being loved by another person. Best to keep spinning, eyes all but closed with palms upturned and empty.

I did not love Tom, not as I had the faceless men who had once filled my shoeboxes to bursting. But I had loved someone telling me I had pretty lips. When he rubbed the sponge hard as a pumice stone against me in the shower, my nipples felt as if he had set them aflame. For weeks afterward as the sensitivity dulled, I missed the pain, which began to assume the reality of a phantom limb still throbbing with feeling. Whereas the ache that took its place swelled like a storm cloud inside me, the rain refusing to break.

When my roommate moved back to Minneapolis, I threw our TV in the dumpster and sat so still on the end of the couch I had taken from the alley that I could feel my pulse in my toes and fingers. I was aware I did not yet know how to spin without becoming dizzy. I sat watching my chest rise and fall as if my lungs collapsing and refilling themselves were building up to something. I looked at a photograph of my grandmother taken before her wedding and began painting.

During the French Revolution, weather vanes with cockerels at their tips displaced all the crucifixes in all the churches as part of a process known as desanctification, as part of ridding the country of religion, though I cannot help regarding it as a holy transformation.

And though I have left off praying for this life entirely, I have spun slowly in the dry August grass, asking the wind at my fingertips for the cockerels' return. I have closed my eyes and wished for the priests to leave the doors open, on either side of the nave and in all seasons, so the breeze will turn the cockerel continually round again, so it will point in no one direction for long. So that inside every house of God there will be a body always at dance, wind blowing it which direction it chooses. A painted metal bird atop an altar with only moving air for a lover. The wind's breath being the closest to the scrape of a falling asteroid the cockerel will come.

The photograph of my grandmother stood luminous and sepia and fading for three weeks on my windowsill. When I handed her my portrait at Easter, she held the canvas loosely from one corner with two fingers. She never framed or hung it, only dropped it in the back of her closet. Poor with color, I'd painted her skin too dark an umber. Yet I had replicated her face's stern ovoid structure, distilled some of her eyes' hazel torpor. Her chin was large in proportion to her cheek bones, her upper lip thin even when younger.

Only her lovers would have overlooked these things. In later years, I knew she had them, one the husband of her only sister living into her eighties, who never spoke to her afterward except for sending a card at Christmas. The more I studied her face and body to render it accurately, the more I realized they would have had much to forgive, large nose and wide hips and flaccid mouse-colored hair that nevertheless kept its curl from the rollers she slept in.

In the end, when her husband took his own mistress and divorced her, she was asked to do the larger share of forgiving, something she delayed for decades, until all such strength she may have had to do so atrophied like the muscles of her arms, into flesh wings incapable of flying. She did little more as I remember than spend whole days in bed smoking cigarettes while reading novels with scrolling gold titles on their covers. Had she forgiven him, she may not have consigned my portrait to the bowels of her closet. Savoring the petrichor of asteroids she had once tempted near her, she would have seen some beauty there, regardless of the painter's ability.

If you whirl yourself with sufficient speed on the dewy summer grass, you can forget you have not been loved enough. You can shed the film that clings to you the same as sap to tree bark, that makes you sticky when you brush against a strange man in an elevator. Yet if you spin slowly as the planet itself, your skin breathes through a layer of nectar too sweet with longing for anyone to suck for overlong. You understand why the most beautiful dervish is the only one to keep his eyes closed, and you no longer wonder about the shape or thinness of your lips. You listen to the lute's silence and are, for a moment, comforted.

Eel Electric

The largest space in the universe is the space inside your head. And inside an astronaut's helmet the space is quieter, which is more of a reason to wear one than even the fact your head would explode in outer orbits if you didn't. Only my Barbie astronaut never wore a helmet over hair the color of bread, and her world was often noisier than she liked it. She never walked inside the Barbie house to lounge on the sofa wedged between the stove and pieless pie cabinet. She didn't prop her feet on a cold burner, displaying a rubber vagina to the tinfoil mouse who lived inside the broiler. She didn't sit topless beneath the hair dryer waiting for Ken, still marooned on an iceberg, as I told the others each day he failed to show again.

She never traveled to the moon either. Instead, she sat on a gable swinging her feet over a polyurethane dormer, wearing her magenta space suit while straining her ears to listen to the gramophone that sat silent upon another Barbie's dresser.

If any Barbie is in danger of committing suicide, it is the one who breathes the least oxygen, the one who feels she must venture to the moon alone, however unlikely that is to happen. Then space travel when you stand only eleven inches tall and always on tiptoe is tantamount to suicide as it is. You're dying either way, only so slowly you have plenty of time to think. And all that space to do it in, between one ear and the other.

My mom had no way of knowing it, but she didn't birth a daughter with eyes and hair so muddy looking no soap could ever clean them. She had hatched an astronaut instead, one with her helmet stowed deep inside her closet, one who could hold her breath just long enough to escape to the moon underwater if there was no alternative.

The Barbie, she might have seen but didn't, was only a toy for me to play with before I became a spacewoman, a toy I taught to hold her breath beneath the bathwater for as long as my mom took to wash my hair clean of what dirtied it. I taught her to play dead below the soap suds collapsing onto my stomach while others clung to the tub's skeleton.

Life was too short to bother living in the Barbie house, I decided. Yet it was still long enough to sit and swing my feet over its rooftop a moment, to dream of a life misspent sleeping in our freezer shaped like a coffin. Only this was not how the end would come, I knew without knowing it for certain, because I sensed even then the end is hotter than life's inception. I wiped perspiration from my face with my shirt's frayed bottom as my mom shouted at me to come help her in the garden.

Too much vegetation and a person can almost forget about the moon's barrenness. So many plants spilled pink fruit into my lap, shooting seeds into my mouth when I held it open. Still the moon hovered above us with its same gray blankness as my mom and I stooped in each other's shadows, filling our buckets with peas and cabbage.

Sometimes I'd look up and watch the pale flaps of my mom's inner thighs secrete a stale jelly. I saw the freckles on her arms were growing darker as the sun leered low in the early morning. I saw both she and the sun were well on their way to dying just as I reached the end of the row and needed to start another—to just keep working, she told me. I picked pods looking swollen to bursting, oblong cysts so pregnant with disease I hardly needed to pull them, only sit and wait for them to rain on top of me.

Sliding my fingernail down a moist pod spine, letting each pea plop into a bowl on our back porch swing, I dreamt of coolness while looking toward the freezer sitting only a few feet away from where we were shelling. I let my dog lick salt pooling between my toes like silt along a sandbar tapering into nothing. The rabbits, my mom lamented, ate more from our garden each evening.

There are less today for picking, she said, than yesterday, and this world, I thought, is not for us, Mommy. The rabbits are chewing all the peas. Best we leave before they chew us next into middens. Sweating on this porch swing, we're wet as fish already flying into a whale's rictus. Let me take us to the cooling place before this life turns hot as a furnace.

Only the cooler's not big enough for both of us, which only means we'll have to drown ourselves inside a lake cool to freezing. You'll have to take both your hands from the steering wheel while unfastening stray rollers you leave in your hair each morning. You'll have to unpin one as we approach a lake large enough to hold both our bodies. You'll have to do this while driving me to kindergarten as I sit in the backseat, loosening my shoelaces.

Once we've started drowning, I'll unroll my window and slip through its lacuna. An eel raging with electricity will sift past me, and I'll grasp its tail while its fins fan themselves like silver-skinned geishas. You'll clasp my ankle, Mommy, and we'll become knotted, you, the eel, and I connected. With the contraction of a single muscle, the eel will wrench you through the half-open window then pull us both through a subaqueous tornado. We'll fall weightless upon sand pulsing like a heart distended, until the eel attenuates into the tail of a kite against a waterborne firmament. Until the darkness encases us beneath a woolen blanket.

I tried to stop breathing in the bathtub while my Barbie astronaut floated up between my knees. I tried but didn't succeed and knew we'd have to find a lake once we left for town to buy milk and packets of wild flower seeds. I decided on the end as soon as I knew an end was coming so I would not drown along the way without my mom beside me. Because that would always be the danger, drowning while living.

She told me there was no need to escape, honey, that God was infinite, in this life and the one to come after. She said we could not leave God's love and we shouldn't want to. Yet I wanted the moon, where there was no God and no oxygen, while my mom hungered for the plenty she thought God provided, not seeing God preferred rabbits. She hungered then sucked violently at a thinning fistula of air the moment my dad unplugged the ventilator. She bit at a pillow instead of grasping my ankle under water. She extended a blue hand to a receding pocket of vapor.

When I was six years old, however, we had nineteen years as yet left together, years when she dressed me in long apricot-colored dresses. Years when the moon shone full enough for her to paint her toenails while sitting with her chin to her knee outside on summer evenings. Years when there was so much living I kept my astronaut helmet stowed on a shelf too high for me to reach and slept with my bedroom window open so I could hear the sweet strum of crickets. Years when I fell asleep chewing bubble gum and my mom cut it out of my hair in clumps large as small mammals in the morning. Years when the crackle of her knees pulling weeds was so soothing a strain, a percussive melisma natural as the music of the spheres mistaken for silence, unheard only because we heard it always. Years when I let myself forget about God and the moon both and took baths in a river too shallow to consider drowning an option. Years when I emerged muddier from the indulgence and walked naked up the bank then dirtied the towel she wrapped me in.

There were years too when I appeared to become a woman rather than a space traveler, as ordinary a vision as any mother could wish of her daughter. Years when I needed instruction only how to cross my legs at dinner rather than career weightlessly across a crater. Years when it was enough that I dry dishes without leaving any spots on them, that I not stain the sheets at night once I began bleeding from the blunt arrow between my legs that time only sharpened.

Yet when the years reached their end, my husband said it was a waste, this constant swallowing of aspirin to try to disappear inside a lake that itself had vanished. I had missed my chance to drown and die beside her when she went before me. I would end by losing my hearing or incurring brain damage, to the point I could no longer read a stop sign but would just keep walking.

My mom had driven into the lake without me, and all I could think was, How long until I follow? I thought this while knowing there was no new planet for us to meet—there were far too many, in even one small galaxy— once I doffed my helmet and fertilized the pea plants for those still going hungry. Yet there is no life without love, I tried explaining, and all the love had gone with her, as I knew it would from the beginning. I lay in bed saying "love, love, love," and nothing else for days, because all the words I heard or said ran together in the same somnolent stream, and I knew she couldn't hear me. I couldn't hear myself either with the tinnitus from the aspirin, but I could say "love" and mean it, to the air at my pillow that grew warmer the harder I exhaled into its softness.

I could say "love" all I wanted but could not escape the fact I was the eel raging electric.

I had been the one to kill her with the contraction of a single muscle, I saw too late and too clearly. I had coaxed her to an early death all along, a way from God and his garden I'd abandoned. I had chosen the moon over her from the time I set my Barbie astronaut's legs swinging over the dormer

My mom wouldn't drive into the lake's center, so I prayed to God the Barbie house would burn down altogether. I prayed and my prayer was too soon answered.

Her last years of life, I unplugged my rotary phone in my studio apartment for whole weekends when I was sure that she would call me, weekends when my neighbors pounded their partners against their bathroom walls, I was pounded a few minutes later, and we all laughed while we opened our mail downstairs together. I poured chocolate syrup woven tightly as a sleeping boa constrictor over ice cream I spooned from paper bowls there was no need of washing. I ate bacon with my fingers without first blotting the grease as she had shown me. I wore bright, hard colors she told me were unflattering.

I thought I was flying to the moon when I was only shutting myself inside another room of the Barbie house all along, resting my legs on a cold burner while displaying my vagina to the tinfoil mouse that lived inside the broiler. Then her cancer burnt down the house along with all the rest of her, and I wandered the city in my space suit, an astronaut with no way of floating any higher, of seeing any more of the galaxy. Floating is still something I can do only in water.

Friends, co-workers, distant cousins said she looked lovely lying in her casket, and I nodded politely. Even I, though, was lovelier than my mom's cadaver, if not enough to count among the living. Not enough to keep breathing just for someone to look at me like a Barbie in a box always smiling and waving.

Yet instead of dying for not being as pretty as I'd like to be or because my mom's no longer here to observe the discrepancy, I've kept working, at a pet rescue magazine that rescues nothing. The rescue fund only keeps the magazine itself from going bankrupt. I've known now for months but still sit here typing.

Because life is barren enough to no longer take much notice of the moon or stars twitching behind it, I sit eight hours a day at my desk beside a succulent plant I bought at a nearby florist, petting it when my fingers feel stiff from so cold an office. Every day I write in the voice of animals missing eyes or limbs, asking someone to give them a home and overlook their bladders' weakness. If no one calls the shelter within a month of publication, the animals are put to a sleep from which no one will wake them. They may not be much prettier than corpses, but that they keep living is deemed important.

132

My lunch, kept all morning in the break room, smells of dog food and hamster dung by noon. There are dogs and hamsters both in this office, and the shit from the hamsters sits around days before anyone dumps it in the garbage. I never offer to take the hamsters home on weekends, as others have noticed, because my apartment is surrounded by rats as it is and I need no more rodents.

This year, my husband and I didn't celebrate or decorate for Christmas. But after the New Year, I bought a string of plastic stars from the White Elephant, which sits next to a Persian restaurant I visit once or twice a month on average. Sahib, its owner, recently died of a heart attack, I learned from a waitress. He gave me free baba ghanoush each time I came in, though I long stopped ordering it because I never liked eggplant to begin with.

I've renamed several shelter dogs Sahib since we met, because I like the name as much as I did the man and his cheek with a mole on it. His was also on his right cheek, the same as mine, which I'll never have removed no matter how large it looks to a dermatologist. Because it resembles a darkened brain with no skull surrounding it. Because it has thoughts of its own, and I don't want to disturb it as I untangle stars knotted tightly as the nerves of a fish flashing with electric current.

Orisons

"You left and I cried tears of blood. My sorrow grows. It's not just that You left. But when You left my eyes went with You. Now, how will I cry?" —*Rumi*

"Honey, you are a baby in this world and don't know how to howl yet."
—*William H. Gass*

A Silent Film

Inside the refrigerator were eight quail eggs crowded on a paper towel I folded into a sailboat. The boat, though, was rudderless so no one could steer it starboard behind the milk. Originally it had looked like a swallowtail with half a broken wing. Only I like boats without engines better than butterflies myself. I like things to move through water when there is no water about.

My 3-year-old nephew told me they were baby chicks. Only I corrected him, reminding him they were unfertilized, that the yolk was only unused placenta, honey muffin. Their poor mama had been celibate all her days, I told him. Never once was she mounted from above and sweetly toppled off her branch. We at length agreed to call them dinosaur eggs certain never to hatch, by way of compromise. Because where would dinosaurs go in a house with ceilings as low as this?

Each egg looked mottled with moles, birthmarks of baby quails never to be conceived. During the four days I spend at my sister and brother-in-law's house, helping them paint lawn furniture pink as pigeon feet, the eggs are never served. My brother-in-law bought them at the farmers' market—for fun, he told me, as if eating them would not also be. As if calling quail eggs dinosaurs caged safely in their shells suffices as sustenance. I make myself eggs for lunch at least twice a week, I say, and have never minded moles. Just look at those upon my face, dark as ants in a blonde wood sea.

They were all hard-boiled before he bought them, by someone who made these chickless eggs too soft for their bones to break. Because it is only brittle things yet to inflate with steam that shatter, whose placenta has yet to thicken into yellow Styrofoam.

I have begun holding my breasts in other people's bathrooms, after I've washed my hands and before I finger-comb my hair so it looks less like a nest of baby birds long flown. These two sacks of flour at my chest like being held, and I am a mother to these two breasts alone. They prefer there to be male hands upon them always, eclipsing each areola with the petroglyph of his palms. I want to hang them over a bannister so the man who climbs the stairway will hold them for me, because they are warm while the house is cold, let's pretend. The man ascending the stairs is wearing a sweater and striped wool socks. His hands reach for the nearest source of heat, when we walk back to the bathroom and lock the door for once, boiling ourselves so we won't break. This happens all year long.

My sister, seven months pregnant with her placenta hanging low near her cervix, does laughing yoga twice a week at an hour better spent writhing through dreams that make me bite my tongue and jackknife my knees. She wakes me at 6 am, when I stumble to her car to learn I can no longer touch my toes, when I see that the skin of the Indian woman who teaches the class has more than half burnt off in patches looking like the relief of continents on a topographical map. Her forehead, otherwise dark as maple bark, is bordered with white like chalk, a nimbus of pain past but present still to those who look. Her arms resemble quail egg shells, however. Skin untouched by fire as yet—where the bark has yet to peel and release its sap—has receded into oblong moles.

As we stretch our arms behind our backs taut as bows poised to fire their arrows, she smiles into my face, which she has never seen. Later, when we laugh, scaring away imaginary sparrows, she smiles still wider, with her mouth ajar, so that a sparrow sparing nothing might fly inside her. The one bird we failed to frighten away, that took our laughter all for pleasure, still poses a danger.

Most laughing exercises involve food we can no more eat than quail eggs nested inside a sailboat made from paper. My sister likes the hot peppers best, which force us to wave our fingers frantically beside our mouths,

138

sniggering with habanero vapor at our throats as we fan our tongues like flames of flesh. But I prefer pouring the buttermilk. I prefer turning sideways, straddling four floorboards while churning by way of transferring milk from one pitcher to another. Buttermilk is less amusing than hot peppers perhaps, certainly to the group at large. I laugh more easily, though, when my tongue is cooled.

The Indian woman, twenty or so years older than myself, can touch her toes with the heel of her hands and probably kiss her elbow too. While my fingers hang slack at my side, I admire my legs anew, their freckled amphorae filled with buttermilk, skin still with the sheen of an egg from whose shell I have yet to break. I regard my ankles' smoothened scythes and trace bruises looking like the footprints of frogs up my calves, the result of any number of collisions with stray furniture legs, which oft impede my route to the kitchen. I never watch where I'm going, people always say, those who see me when I cannot see myself, when there is no bathroom mirror to watch me holding these twin pendulums that swing only when I'm running.

Yet what pretty legs these are, which I rarely bother to notice, because the only mirror in my apartment ends at my navel. I would have a far prettier face if I could, had I only the option. But at least I have these two legs, which I can see any time I please, whenever I take the time to bend my nose down to my knees.

My sister and brother-in-law try three times to make me watch a silent film, one in which Buster Keaton goes west, forsaking his small Indiana town. Playing a ranch hand named Friendless, Buster befriends a heifer playing Brown Eyes as herself, with whom he drives a herd of cattle through downtown Los Angeles. They keep telling me I'll love it, that I'll laugh and laugh and laugh, but I never do sit through it. I ate too many peppers too early that morning to sit still for long, I tell them. I stay standing at the kitchen counter instead, waiting for dinosaurs to hatch.

I never see Friendless don his devil costume to scare the cows into the L.A. abattoir and save his ranch at movie's end. Instead, I mention while helping to clean the house for the party they are hosting, that I am far too friendless myself to find it as funny as I should, a woman with brown eyes and pretty urn legs set for the slaughterhouse. At this they titter weakly while I laugh again as if I'm pouring buttermilk. Silent films, I tell them too, are never really silent. They are only unfertilized eggs, waiting for the talkies to come.

I cannot sleep here, where only the frogs make any noise at night and whose footprints leave bruises. My sister is concerned though tired herself when I tell her I fall asleep only after her son has wakened, that I sleep no more than three hours through the night. Normally, though, I sleep seven. In my Chicago apartment, where the sirens never cease, I have no shortage of energy.

I have not cried for nine months, I tell her, and maybe this is too long a time. I could have had a child within this stretch if I'd only wanted. Our parents died nine years ago, and she thinks I ought to cry about their absence perhaps more often, if only to restore my REM to a less disruptive rhythm. So I cry in the kitchen while her son spoons cereal down his shirt. I cry as if I am at crying yoga while she tells my nephew, who stares with his mouth agape and leaking milk, that everyone gets sad sometimes. Aunt Melissa is fine, though, we all trust. I nod to confirm this while feeling the heat rising from my nipples, boiling so they won't break when the man on the stairs lets his arms fall to his pockets.

I sleep upstairs, in the guest bedroom papered with pine and smelling of the forest razed to build this dwelling. I wrap my body in a blanket my mom knitted the year I was born, she told me. It is blue and white and chevron and unspeakably soft. It is the blue of clouds ready to rain their torrents, while the patches of white have yellowed into the color of Indian

140

skin burnt at its esophagus. Still a warmth resides there apart from the temperature of the room. I open the window wide to sleep and wrap the blanket tightly around my hips, hot to boiling as I am, knowing I can sleep long later in the week among the sirens.

Next morning, my sister's friend Jane brings more tables and chairs for me to paint for the party next evening, to celebrate the end of the summer and the baby girl to come. I walk outside and pretend to try to wrest the hose from my nephew's grip and hear Jane sigh and say her husband's drinking has added an easy fifty pounds since my sister last saw him.

Aaron teaches high school English, and I have met him only once. He has drunk and slept the summer away, Jane admits, thinking I cannot hear her above the hose's hiss. She has sunlight hair snaking down her coccyx, and her skin luminesces like enamel apples at dawn. Jane is planning his meals to control his weight, she says to regain control herself, to keep the sun from setting and giving the moon a chance.

Wiping shards of grass off my legs and pretending I haven't heard, I tell them both I am playing the gong in a gamelan ensemble whose music has no words. I've played several Indonesian instruments looking like bronzed xylophones now for weeks though prefer the gong. And my teacher is such a beautiful specimen. He has to remind me not to play it too hard when I end the song.

This makes them both uncomfortable, I see by the veins swelling in their necks, this openly finding another man desirable who is not your husband. Their silence only makes me tell them my teacher's eyes are almost violet. He has endless legs and fingers just as long. I have seen his pupils dilate when I take off my shoes to step over the instruments we play always on the carpet. He is moving to Java, though, I confess, as if this is the world's end. As if the teacher taking his place doesn't also have purple irises.

My nephew has taken to swallowing water from the hose three or more hours in a day. He holds it in his cheeks and then he spits it out, like a cherub in a fountain somewhere in Western Europe. This must be natural, my brother-in-law observes. Boys filling their mouths with water in the old country must have impressed artists with their inflated faces. I laugh, conceding my nephew's seraphic appearance, he who does the same at night in the tub.

Better to swallow fire than just keep spitting water out, I respond, a little tired of watching this. I tell my brother-in-law all the gargoyles on all the world's cathedrals derived from only one. A legendary bishop of Rouen had once tried to burn a dragon. Only finding the dragon resistant to fire after it had spat and swallowed so much prior, the bishop instead beheaded the serpent. He mounted it above the drainpipe of his house of worship, where the head funneled rain and protected the masonry in the process.

A cherub ornamenting a fountain and a grotesque nailed to a cathedral are more closely related than you might imagine, I say, while my brother-in-law politely listens. Only one is young and one isn't. One swallows water for fun and the other under harness. If his son keeps swallowing the hose water, in other words, he'll eventually become a dragon.

He tells me he has come across this of late, this concept of eating fire or water, as it may be—both can do equal damage to a building—only to eat some more of it. He doesn't elaborate, so I clarify this signals pain's acceptance, that perhaps he heard it from me, who makes metaphors a topic of conversation far too often. Then he tells me what a good aunt I am, that I still might become a mother if I do so quickly. I smile and shake my head, thinking only that the earth has yet to spit out my own parents like water from a fountain, that for this a large part of me is still waiting. Only it's not their absence keeping me awake while my nephew is sleeping. It's these breasts that no one holds, that smash against the bed.

When my husband arrives that evening to also celebrate the baby-to-be, he cups my hips and walks his fingers down my sternum while I open the refrigerator door, looking for eggs to eat. I push him away among so much company then sit apart from him while rewatching the beginning of *Go West*. My sister shouts that I am Brown Eyes to make me sit and stay, to watch Buster Keaton. My sister has brown eyes as well, bigger and deeper than my own. She also looks more bovine now she is so near to birthing. I stand up to wash the dishes, saying so much ragtime music rattles my nerves, which have become brittle as egg shells on so little sleep for so many nights on end. I remind everyone I have missed my gamelan class for this long weekend.

My brother-in-law mutes the volume on the silent film and types "gamelan" into his laptop to play a song without any real melody to soothe me, a song that changes its tempo at the drummer's discretion. My husband then interrupts the music, professing to the air spiraling from the ceiling fan above us that I am in love with my teacher, he who plays the drums. He says it only because it's so far from being true. Because we both wonder if I'm still in love with him and, if not with my teacher, then with whom.

When Aaron walks onto the deck for the party with Jane behind him, he is carrying green bean casserole. I hug them both, set the dish on a folding chair, and unwrap it of foil. I sit and pour then drink some wine with them while we watch my nephew puff his cheeks with water from the hose. They start giggling when I explain he only does this so he can spit it out. If he had to drink the water, he would hardly bother with the whole business. Still they're best to avoid that region of the yard, I remind them, with ground so soft you can sink in mud ankle deep. He runs in circles spraying my sister until the hose gets a kink.

Next morning, my sister and I make tomato pie. She takes filo dough from the freezer, and we shake flour onto the counter and roll out the pastry crust, thin enough to overspread the pan like a layer of epidermis. The recipe tells us to weight it with bags of beans to keep the crust from bubbling while it cooks, but my sister has no beans in her cupboard. I suggest we forget this part, that what's a little bubbling to us? But she says we ought to find a substitute, that did the bubbling not amount to a hill of beans the recipe would hardly read as such. She then pours rice over the sheet of foil atop the crust, saying this should work. Yet when we take it out of the oven, one side has risen higher and become browner than the other. The rice has slid down deeper into the earth, slumping toward the sinkhole my nephew deepens with his hose water.

We layer tomatoes and cheese over the uneven crust, weighting the fruit more heavily on the side risen over the pan's edge while Friendless corrals his cattle once more. I complain of the noise coming from the silent film again, reminding my brother-in-law I have herded cattle enough on my own lost farm while my dad was funnier than Buster Keaton. My sister deftly redirects conversation, recalling when I used to cook only scrambled eggs and nothing more, serving them on Sunday mornings for a table set for four. When the sound of crunching echoed from one plate to another, because I always left some eggshells in, never cracking them all the way open. Because I never watch what I'm doing, she adds, smiling as I bump my knee against the oven door.

Only eyes can see themselves. The rest of the body cares nothing for its own appearance or that of anything else. My legs have remained indifferent to their shape, however many frog bruises scale my thighs, trying to reach my pubis. Touch alone suffices for all our other parts, those without any irises.

On the train to our apartment from O'Hare, I sit beside a man wearing a fez, closer to him than to my husband, who is on my other side. He projects his voice to the woman seated across from him, complaining that the plane's air conditioning vent, the one above his head, rained his whole flight. Crystallized beads of air kept melting on his book, so he hardly read the whole time. The woman laughs, dismisses this. But I want to sound my gong for silence then interject that I had the same problem, this air turning fast to rain inside the plane. The conductor then announces we have to exit at the next stop, that from there we can either take a bus or start walking.

Standing on the platform, I wait for the crowd to thin before descending the stairs behind my husband. I watch two pigeons mate on a beam above the tracks. Were one not pressing down on top of the other's back, I would not know which sex was which. They look so much the same, neither one with breasts for someone to hold should she rest them on a ledge. Yet from this simple act lasting only a few seconds, she will hatch some eggs in some corner of some train track. If they fall, their shells will break against a sidewalk fossilized with gum. These few and fragile baby chicks you might as well eat as not.

Airplanes over Disneyland

In the mid-1990s, a hippopotamus swallowed a dwarf during a circus accident in northern Thailand. The dwarf bounced sideways off a trampoline as a hippo named Hilda was yawning, bored with the trapeze artists. Of course no such thing happened, as myriad news outlets reported. Just another Internet hoax, as happens all too often. Yet hippos and dwarfs still exist, if more so the latter. Because hippos live only in sub-Saharan Africa apart from zoos and circuses, while dwarfs are found everywhere except within the maw of a hippopotamus. People who can grow only so tall live on all seven continents, which is to say all of us. The average hippo grows to 13 feet, making us all dwarfs in comparison.

For my sixteenth birthday, Laura gave me a folder emblazoned with a unicorn with a rainbow stamped on its rear end after we'd changed into our gym clothes for fourth period, to play volleyball without really playing it, to avoid the ball on purpose to save bruising our wrists. Inside the folder was a sheet of paper on which a poem began, "Airplanes at night, and I'm on the Peter Pan ride at Disneyland," and ended, "And she can see me, knowing I, like her, will always be there." I remember no more lines for certain, only that Laura had written it all with a crayon the color of a hippopotamus ensconced in chlorine. The her to which the narrator was referring looked down on the narrator from the window of a plane throughout, it seemed. Yet this other girl appeared explicitly only at poem's end. How they saw each other at such a distance I never fathomed.

And though I can quote no more lines than this verbatim, I remember the narrator went on to limn her own reflection, an almost woman still with a child's stature. She had Laura's same auburn hair and floated through Neverland on a pirate galleon. Still I never knew whether the narrator was Laura herself beyond question, because my hair also resembles wheat begun to burn in autumn. Who might have been at play in the theme park and who was only looking down from above while traveling to another destination, then, remains an open question. Laura was much shorter than me, yet from an airplane's height you can hardly tell the difference between dwarfs and those whose height is only average. I have always assumed as well that Laura could have hardly known herself whether she sat in a commercial airliner or a pirate ship overlooking a land of eternal children.

Hippos are largely herbivorous, feeding solely on soft grasses, reeds, and ferns. So even did the dwarf bounce inside Hilda's mouth from the trampoline, the dwarf more than likely survived, dying decades later from natural causes. The dwarf would have been regurgitated as Hilda sprayed the unicyclists with excess saliva they might have drowned in—an ancillary tragedy that went unreported. If anyone had swallowed a dwarf in Thailand, it would have been a werewolf or something like it, a species born to devour prey bouncing high as the rafters solely to entertain the audience. Unlike hippos, werewolves are carnivorous. They feast freely on humans. Their ripe, red hearts and other internal organs.

In Iron Age Europe, lycanthropy served as a metaphor for initiation into the warrior classes. Men trained to develop blood thirst for anyone of another race or country, whereas other civilizations conceived of the process more literally. The Greek geographer Pausanias wrote that Zeus transformed Lycaon into a wolf because he had murdered an infant, while Pliny quotes Agriopas regarding a tale of a man turned lupine after tasting a dead baby's entrails and liking their taste. Similarly, northern Europeans once believed those who died in mortal sin returned to earth as werewolves with a thirst for human hemoglobin, something I may have done in my innocence without knowing.

When we were both seven, Audrey told me to drink three raw egg yolks for five consecutive days after school to avoid becoming a werewolf, as others had done before me. The egg yolks, she said, would keep hair from sprouting all over my skin, the first sign of transforming into something certain to eat my parents. At the time, she was my best friend. A few years later, though, she became Laura's when we all went to the same junior high school, when we had almost forgotten how close we once were to becoming cannibals, no longer quite human.

Even after I had swallowed more than a dozen egg yolks along with their albumen, my hair kept growing from out every pore, I noticed. I ran my hands along all my body's edges then felt inside some orifices. Finding fuzz growing inside my ears all of a sudden, I knew Audrey's cure had come too late. I had no tendriling of pubic hair as yet or any hair growing from my armpits. Still what hair I had portended I would change species.

It was only lycanthropy, not death, Audrey said when I ran to her crying and helpless at recess. My dad had hung a new swing from the magnolia tree outside our kitchen, I still supplicated, as if this fact alone might reverse the process. He had cut the seat from a fallen rafter once supporting our barn's ceiling. He had given me room to grow as my legs kicked higher into its blossoms. I hated to punish him by sinking my fangs into his carotid artery.

I had no choice, though, it seemed. With fifteen egg yolks down my gullet, my legs were still swathed in hair growing long and golden. I was leaving my family while being swallowed by the spirit of an animal I had only lately known existed. I lived in fear for a couple more months, until I knew the truth for certain. Were it not another hoax, I would have died so much shorter a person.

After school, I often trailed Audrey and Todd, her cousin, to their grandmother's basement, which lay next door to my Aunt Millie's, where I waited for my mom to finish work and drive me back to our farm, ten miles south of the town where Audrey and I went to Catholic school. Playing a Def

148

Leppard cassette, they unzipped their jeans. They rubbed their underwear against each other in too early of frottage while telling me to watch so no one else entered. Todd's leg arched over Audrey's back while their grandmother made us lemonade upstairs by the pitcher.

Audrey, I knew from slumber parties at her home on the town's outskirts, had a stepfather with a sagging red mustache and an outdoor toilet nothing more than a hole in the ground framed by a pink shower curtain hung from a wreath of maple branches. When she spent the night with me, at a place bucolic in comparison, she mimicked being a lion plundering our livestock. She shook her long blonde bangs over her eyelashes and roared at our sheep, until their bleats became shrieks of panic and a fusillade of turds sprayed out their rectums. I followed behind and roared just a little, hoping the sheep would still allow me near them. I hoped the ewes would again permit me to cradle their lambs once Audrey had gone home to pee among the insects.

I never did develop the taste for the blood of humans that Audrey predicted. And though the raw eggs didn't prevent hair from growing everywhere except my palms and the back of my feet, they did halt the final transformation. I grew no sharper teeth and ate none of my family. I never grew large enough to swallow someone as small as Laura, who at sixteen still rode on rides made for children.

Waiting to be assigned teams for volleyball in gym, one day I told Laura that Audrey had once convinced me I was becoming a werewolf. I mentioned that the egg yolks made me vomit, weakening my stomach so I had trouble eating for days on end. That I believed her, she said, though, made sense. I was still so innocent.

Male werewolves, Audrey knew through experience by the time she was seven, had talons that held their penises erect as missiles, poised to impale little girls with limp hair like mine colored like a sunset. A whole gang of werewolves, she insisted, had invaded her bedroom time and again, when she told the leader I soon would join them. She whispered this to me at recess as I wrapped my arms around a water pipe. As a handball game played on beside us, I felt the warmth of the rushing fluid.

More than a hundred mummified dwarfs and skeletons are preserved among modern Egyptology collections. Tableaus depicting dwarfs along tomb walls remain common excavations, as a form of dwarfism known as achondroplasia pervaded the ancient civilization. The dominant genetic mutation carries a 50-percent chance of being passed onto offspring, and translations of hieroglyphs reveal that Egyptian dwarfs suffered little prejudice compared to what they do at present, when we love to watch them tumble into the jaws of death during a circus. Egypt welcomed very few barbarians and had to suffer the consequences of little genetic variation. In times gone by, everyone was also shorter, in part because of poorer nutrition. We all grow taller, it seems, with hindsight and the inertia that carries us forward.

Even the tallest person, however, only grows so tall for so long a time. Eventually we all are buried where our height hardly matters. This is assuming we don't return as werewolves, that is, drinking the blood of our friends and feasting on their organs. Because of all things there should be an end. People should grow only so high. One person should dwarf another by only so many inches, so we remain certain we are all the same species. So we can rest assured that, when one of us dies, there is another to replace us who looks reasonably similar from a distance. A species who will not prey on our descendants.

Of the three of us during our sophomore year of high school, Audrey stood the tallest. Laura was so short she was almost a dwarf by comparison, while I was of no height at all. I stood so much in the middle as to go unnoticed.

Yet whatever their disparity in height, Laura and Audrey both wore frayed denim shorts in autumn, spring, and summer, shorts with so little fabric you could see the hang of their buttocks. Both smoked pot on swing sets and made out with boys I only lusted after beneath the bleachers. My parents knew Audrey from our time together as children, but they never did meet Laura. They never looked into her cornflower eyes or wondered how she kept her tube tops from sliding waistward while she swung her arms high enough to keep pace with the longer legs of everyone around her. Laura and I likely would not have stayed friends much longer. Still I kept her poem folded in a book and threw away the folder. That and a watch from my parents were all the presents I received for my birthday, which fell on the last day of school so no one else remembered. Both told time, and both I've since lost track of.

I was home reading the Saturday night when Audrey and some boy driving her stepfather's corvette inched Laura's boyfriend's jeep forward from behind while Laura sat shotgun. The jeep tipped over on its left axis when the prodding vehicle's front tires failed to align with the jeep's back ones. Laura flew from her perch a few feet right of the wheel and lapsed into a coma for five months, before her parents consented to have her taken off a ventilator at the doctor's counsel. Although I never knew Laura as well as Audrey, I had reason to believe, from the many hours I sat in the hospital throughout that summer, she had never actually looked out the window of an airplane, over Disneyland or anywhere else. Her parents drove an old van with a rusted bumper from which their license plate hung by a clothes hanger.

I took my place at her bedside with ease I hardly understood from her coma's inception, holding her doll-like hand with the possession of old friendship when ours had only started. When our gym teacher made me sit on the side of the pool for turning back flips underwater when I was supposed to be rescuing a drowning dummy, Laura had excused herself because of sudden cramps and we sat together, laughing at the flailing inflated arms until we were separated. I didn't smoke pot or give anyone head under any bleachers, but I could turn back flips instead of rescuing someone hardly human. I could quaff four successive slurpies at lunch until the brain freezes started. I could slide down steel banisters and bruise my shins. I could paint the bed of my dad's pickup truck into a bottomless ocean and speak with the gargly voice of a scuba diver during roll call for volleyball. And Laura had laughed at it all, though she was hardly full grown herself and could only grow so tall. She was exactly two weeks younger than me and four or five inches shorter. Had she have lived to adulthood, a hippo would have swallowed her.

Audrey hardly ever came to the hospital as I remember. She gave me in this way without knowing it more time to stare at Laura's fulvous eyelids, crusted with pus I blotted with a tissue I wetted with saliva.

Audrey's younger brother, Dustin, had a form of childhood cancer that had stunted his growth from the time he was a toddler, and he never did grow enough hair to cover his skull altogether. In kindergarten, he looked like a balding old man instead of a boy whose hair grew in a patchworked pattern. For several years, his smooth egg head budded a new lump every month or so, and we were forced to pray for him after saying the Pledge of Allegiance. Some lumps looked purple as bruises, while others were the same color as his face, fleshy volcanoes that might and might not blow us all to pieces.

I always considered him highly intelligent, though he was probably babbling his alphabet no sooner than average. Only he looked so much younger, wise for his years when he really wasn't, because his legs had never grown, only his head, out of all proportion. I realized this while watching him play video games as I sat in Audrey's kitchen, overlooking the outdoor toilet with the pink shower curtain while waiting for my mom to pick me up from another slumber party for a girl who talked to werewolves on a regular basis.

The end of Laura's life did not measurably affect my own aside from making me a little sadder than I was already. It allowed me to leave school the afternoon of the funeral and eat fast food instead of the same chicken fried steak the cafeteria served every Wednesday. I acquired a token suffering and made vast erroneous assumptions about my own capacity for pain in the process. Unlike Audrey, Laura had never punished me for my innocence, yet once she was gone I didn't miss her. She had written me only one poem about airplanes over Disneyland I thought childish. Neither of us knew who was the real narrator.

Peter Pan himself made no appearance in the Peter Pan ride constructed by Walt Disney's original team of engineers. As the ride's passengers flew from London to Neverland, they witnessed everything except the eponymous boy who never grew or perished. Later the masses expressed their disappointment, though the designers had intended for guests to inhabit Peter's perspective. That no one had understood this tells sorely on the human condition if you think about it. No one who had ridden the ride had ever loved someone else enough to see the world from inside of his or her skin, had ever escaped their own integument to rest wholly within that of another person. Trying to see yourself from another's perspective, though, proves just as fruitless. You can see yourself in a mirror, yes, but you tug your right ear when it's actually your left. You can never strap yourself inside the Peter Pan ride and watch yourself staring down the pirates. You must either be the girl at Disneyland or the girl flying over it.

In 1983, after decades of service, engineers at last put Peter inside the action so park patrons could observe rather than become him for the space of a few minutes. People could fly over London and then cross into a timeless dimension while watching Peter fly alongside them. Animatronic, he could also narrate and explain their experience for them. Yet his speeches proved repetitive.

Laura, I assumed, wrote her poem from a vintage perspective, overlooking Disneyland 1982 or before it. She thought when you rode the Peter Pan ride you never saw Peter but instead became him, an eternal boy typically played on stage by a young woman no taller than Laura at sixteen, as grown as she would get. It was the mid-90s, and she was also the one who told me a dwarf had been swallowed by a hippopotamus. At first, I believed her. She laughed and nodded.

The last time I saw Audrey was in a church parking lot after my mom's funeral when we were 26 and she stood uttering her condolences, bouncing a baby on her hip with some impatience while trying to burp him. We faced each other at eye level, though, I noticed. Perhaps I had grown a few inches since high school, but I always remembered her as a whole head taller, her nose pointed like an arrow at a world that to me was imperceptible. She told me I looked different, but she looked just the same, I offered.

J.M. Barrie based the character Peter on his older brother, who died in an ice-skating accident the day he turned thirteen. A shorter life is an easier life, however, and I continue to fail to see why people fear theirs ending, though their fear perhaps explains Peter Pan's popularity. Most of us are not dwarfs fit for the circus, though all lives may feel short when drawing toward their close. And I may be the first to feel my life has been long enough when the time comes, though perhaps I've also spent too much time only riding in an airplane. Perhaps there is less to be missed from a life overlooking everyone else at play in the theme park below, where the rides grow progressively more lifelike, where the characters converse in programmed monologues.

The airplanes are flying at night, however. The park should be closed, the gates long locked to the public. No one should be riding the Peter Pan who flies over London? Of course it is Laura. It is the same young woman who wore such short shorts with her buttocks flapping underneath them at such a close distance from her ankles. If you saw her only from the back when we were friends, you might mistake for a child of nine or ten, Dustin's slightly older sister in place of his older sister's best friend. Meanwhile I am riding overhead, knowing we will each be here always, she said. Only I am crossing time zones, she only pretending to in a child's ride that travels the same ellipse, so close to the ground she can nearly touch the pirate's handkerchiefs. I am flying to someplace real, to real London perhaps.

Only someone like Laura who spent her sixteenth birthday in a coma would bother breaking into a theme park after hours, though. I stayed home reading and didn't hear of the accident until the morning after she lost consciousness.

Until Audrey told me I was turning into a werewolf, I hadn't noticed I had hair inside my ears or any fuzz swirling around my navel, which I also probed. Even after I realized she was enacting an elaborate ruse and I was becoming no human predator, I remained newly aware of myself as an animal. My hair kept growing longer while darkening in hidden places. I was growing into a body Peter Pan never knew.

Smaller animals tend to live shorter lives than those that are larger. Hippopotamuses average 36 years of existence, pygmy hippos only 27. The median life of a dwarf, however, is the same as that of a taller person. That of those not dwarfs but shorter than average whose boyfriends' jeeps are tipped over by friends by accident is 16 years and a few weeks more. That of their friends in gym class remains to be seen, however. At the moment, I am 35 and could go on longer but won't make a fuss if I live no more than the average hippopotamus. I have never ridden the Peter Pan ride at Disneyland and will likely never bother.

When I was seven and a half and hirsute to the point I knew I was no longer human, I crawled out of bed one night close to ten or eleven and told my mom I was leaving her forever. I asked her to pass the news along to my dad, who was watching basketball one room over. I had done everything I could to stay here as their daughter, but there was no helping it. I was almost a werewolf. Now I had to pack a suitcase and write a note to my sister explaining my disappearance.

My mom walked me back to my bed and told me werewolves were not real, not only invisible, as at first I insisted. She said I would swing from the magnolia tree as long as I wanted, but in this she was lying. Audrey laughed next day at recess when I told her I would remain a little girl until I was a woman. I was too relieved to be angry, relieved and yet sadder. Because of Dustin, who died a few years later without growing any taller. Because of Audrey's outdoor toilet and because of all the dwarfs who are never swallowed and die adult deaths looking like old children.

The Salt Mines

In summers almost too long gone by to too clearly remember, I drank so much water from the hose I asked my mom if I could die of drinking too much. She told me no when weeding our garden, when transferring a band of sweat from her forehead onto her wrist. Realizing my question was not important, I put the hose back in my mouth, allowing water to collapse down my trachea in the process, hoping this might help to smoothen its ridges. I imagined the water rushing over them like waves upon rocks speckling a beach with lumpy bodies of beiges. Regardless of what she said, I still felt drowning in my own skin was an option. I loved my mom but knew her to be oblivious to dying's more common causes.

And then she was no scientist. Later, I realized she'd never heard of water intoxication to begin with. I hadn't heard of such a thing either then, at eight or nine or ten, but sensed my blood should be saltier, weighted with something heavier than water, while she drank only Tab and instant coffee, hot even in August. Looking back, I see it's little wonder she dismissed the danger of thirst overstretching the bladder to near rupture.

Too much water can desalinate your blood so quickly your heart floods and goes the way of minnows eaten by a dolphin. Too little salt and all your cells become waterlogged while your blood-brain barrier is a barrier no longer. For a time, your skin accommodates the influx. You swell as if you've overeaten, becoming rounded as a penguin and walking just as labored with your bloated abdomen. Your neurons, though, have no space to grow inside your skull. Your brain expands then all its electricity darkens.

Although she spent little time teaching me to cook anything elaborate, my mom still reminded me to salt my meat on occasion. She said that without it, steak tasted insipid. Only I've often since forgotten and never noticed a difference. I don't bother cooking steaks, however, only chili with hamburger, to which I add so many jalapenos my eyes begin to water, allowing me to cry under cover for my long lost mother.

And after my crying is finished, I drink more water to replace that which I've just shed forever. I attempt to intoxicate myself with it in the privacy of my kitchen, which overlooks an abortion clinic where protestors gather. They scream for babies unborn to them or any other women while I drain yet more glasses of water, something I've done more times than I ought to admit to anyone who might care to keep me here longer. I hold in my urine while drinking nine glasses so quickly in succession I begin belching over the sirens drowning out the pro-lifers, thinking this death at least will be painless, thinking this as if I've already died several times before in comparison. Thinking this way there will be no blood to clean up afterward.

Blood, though, leaking from steaks' muscle fibers I thought was only juice when younger. I slurped it from my plate after finishing my dinner. Both blood and juice, however, consist of mostly water. Blood is more than half straw-colored plasma, water enriched with enzymes and salt to transport hormones.

Yet however pure it seems besides darker-looking liquids, you're not supposed to drink either plasma or water from a fountain meant for decoration, the latter owing to its chlorine concentration, though a certain amount of chlorine is necessary to kill microorganisms. Without it, none of us would drink water from the tap and survive the experience. More studies, however, link consumption of chlorine to climbing rates of cancer. As if they were low for starters.

So you are not advised to drink from the Trevi Fountain, originally built for this express purpose and not for tourists to take pictures. Its source remains an aqueduct installed by Marcus Agrippa, though now its water is heavily chemically treated as well as recirculated. If you throw a coin in, the fountain will quickly clean it, making it sparkle as it floats to its bottom. The water is too clean, however, for our digestive systems.

Anita Ekberg, who played Sylvia in *La Dolce Vita*, died not long ago and I have yet to see the movie that made her famous. She is recorded as saying her only regret in life was having no children. I cannot claim a similar longing, though when I'm on my deathbed and surrounded by only nurses, I may warm to the sentiment. For now, I'd only like to resemble her in a black strapless and have as many lovers. If only I had kissed a man as she had within the Trevi's waters.

When I was a junior in college studying on the outskirts of Rome with the term nearly ended, I woke one morning realizing I had yet to see the Trevi. Later that night, without a map and struggling to navigate the city by feel alone, I gave up hope of ever finding Neptune on his throne. Knowing better than to ask Italian men for directions, I shuffled back to the bus stop to return farther north to campus.

I was wearing a summer dress I'd bought in Trastevere a few days before this. It was sleeveless with large red roses imprinted over white fabric. Inside it, I felt an approximation of a real Italian woman, as close to being Anita Ekberg, who was Swedish, as I could hope to come. When Massimo first spoke to me from behind, an embodied shadow with legs like an ibis, he whispered, You seem strange, to which I didn't bother responding. Yes, there's definitely something strange about you, he said again, when I turned around to face him. You're American. I can tell by the way you dress, he said smiling, pleased with his assessment.

Not long afterward, we circled the nearby piazza. He bought me a scoop of gelato and told me he was leaving soon to work for an architectural firm in Berlin. But he would miss this, he said gesturing toward Neptune's baying cavalry. He would miss this beauty, he repeated, when I felt the brush of his lips against a cheek I turned against him.

He asked two, three times for my phone number, but I refused him.

Leaving me hours later at the bus stop where he'd first taken my hand as if I'd offered it, he said, I can't make you do what you don't want to, and walked away, attenuating into the shadow of a firefly begun to blink out of existence. Had I only drunk enough water from the Trevi Fountain when I had the chance, I could have died when the promise of love was more real than its absence.

In 2007, a vandal made the Trevi run red for several hours on end, soiling water so clean it kills all algae. He inundated it with a red liquid still to be determined, when some blood looked spilled, to no lasting damage. Had it come from a steak, I would have slurped it. Had Massimo only appeared again to give me directions.

Everyone has, no matter how otherwise unintelligent, the sense to eat when they're hungry, to masturbate when they're horny if no one will fuck them. The body possesses its own intelligence regardless of your will or not to live. If you're thirsty then, drink and dilute your blood's salt content. You have little chance of dying from it whatever you might wish, whereas too much salt in the body makes your blood pressure skyrocket. Your blood panics and runs to exhaustion.

The Dead Sea is six times saltier than the oceans, a place known for inducing relaxation. Although you'll find no fish, several types of bacteria flourish within its depths as well as a single species of algae. Meanwhile we float like a cork dropped in dishwater once we dive in. Because the Dead Sea is denser than our bodies, inside it we grow buoyant. Still every year the sea level falls 13 or more inches. Every year, we float more easily in water that itself is sinking.

With spiritual enlightenment, the body too begins to lighten, becoming more buoyant. So say those who have risen to higher levels of consciousness, those whose egos have dissolved into liquid, leaving all the salt behind them. So say those who feel more like a duck gliding on water's

160

surface than a coin sinking to its bottom, those who have realized the ultimate yet are fuller of emptiness. And emptiness is something I've tried to embrace but have had no luck grasping. Even water feels heavy in comparison, because water has a weight to it. Swim down too deep in the ocean and it crushes your bones into powder resembling salt from a distance.

Many Israelis make their living working in desalination, reaping a large profit. They sell their byproduct at a premium because the salt comes from the Holy Land, meaning an area holier than other places, meaning salt is somehow allied with something sacred, with keeping steak from tasting insipid. Among early Christians, catechumens also ingested salt before receiving baptism. Before being blessed with holy water, the bodies of young Christians were all properly seasoned. Even God, in other words, eats meat every so often. When we're alone in the shower, he keeps his eyes open.

And all this effort we make to live a little longer, curing meat and trying to keep it from rotting in our refrigerators. I often wonder if it's worth it. I often wonder even while, left to itself, my body refuses to consider other options. Hunger's clamor can begin to deafen when accessing higher levels of awareness.

Would my bones float in a bathtub? If only they were lighter. If only they were eaten with holes from cancer like those of my dear, sweet mother. As of this moment, my skull alone might bob at water's surface were the tub well salted. As of this moment, my head has so many holes it's almost useless, though some think even these insufficient.

Ancient Incan skulls reveal several holes carved half an inch in diameter. The lacunae are evidence of Peruvian trephining, the world's oldest surgical procedure. Most anthropologists agree the holes served as portals to allow gods and spirits of loved ones to visit, making the body more porous to numinous experience. Yet if you make too large of one or drill too quickly, the brain's light darkens. Too much emptiness—too wide a doorway for spirits to enter your nervous system—and you yourself vanish.

Were your diet too bereft of sodium, your muscles could neither contract nor soften while your nerves could relay no electrical impulses. This is what comes of salt uneaten. You'd have no more sex, and this world would have no babies in it. We all would die before we were born and then became enlightened, before we watched protestors gather outside abortion clinics as we sat cross-legged above in levitation.

She said, He's sleeping even when he's crying. She was a young mother eating with what looked like her own mom by their similar shape of noses at the table beside me. She sat so near me that my buttocks brushed her shoulders when I slid out to use the toilet. When I came back, they were talking about 401(k)s and financial goals they'd set. And I thought, What about the crying baby? Why is money more important?

When my sister and I went to Peru a year and a half after our mom was buried and our dad soon after that, we spent an afternoon in the salt mines near Ollantaytambo. We followed our guide on a trail so narrow I felt sure I'd lose my balance. I all but knew I'd stumble into a salt pit that would preserve me for the cannibals or God himself if he was interested. Somehow, though, I didn't.

Those women we met working within what resembled the Dead Sea drained of water completely appeared ancient from their faces' creases. We assumed they were elderly and had to keep working because of lifelong poverty. Then we noticed they were carrying babies in slack papooses. Our guide saw our confusion and explained they were our same age or younger, 28 years old at the oldest. He said salt was an aging agent then walked on ahead. But didn't salt keep flesh from rotting? I wanted to ask but couldn't catch up with him. Shouldn't these old young mothers look much younger than the average? I had no answers, only a hypothesis that from the Fountain of Youth springs saltless water. As well as making you look younger, it can also help end your life faster.

And what is it about old women drinking wine, like the mother of the younger mother worried about her savings? Why am I repulsed when they drain a glass in front of me? Why shouldn't they enjoy getting a little drunk and have a headache next morning? I am hardly young myself any longer. I've spent some time in the salt mines, though while carrying no baby.

If I did any financial planning—any beyond planning to kill myself when I have no more money—I might drink wine too more often and celebrate this living. Money, though, doesn't consume too much of salt miners' thinking, I'm guessing. By the end of the day, they're too tired to do more than fall on top of another body and make another baby who will age prematurely.

Today I walked through a tunnel painted white while trodding a blanket of whiter snow beneath. It was a cathedral of whiteness, and I felt my old instinctive longing for purity, for being a person so empty some spirits might fly through me. I ached for my own emptiness, for blood so pure it ran to clarity, so I could see the salt within it sparkling, salt looking like snow that refused to melt as it fell onto my sleeve. Yet when I opened my mouth to the snow still falling, it was tasteless.

Scientists consider water the least toxic compound nature gives us, the closest we can come to grasping emptiness while drinking something that sustains us. Even water, though, can become poison, they acknowledge with reluctance. Were I only athletic and more inclined to sweat, I'd have a better shot at overconsumption, because this is whom most warnings of water intoxication target. I'd dilute my body's salt content in the course of my normal exertions. I'd induce a tidal wave for the sheer exhilaration of turning from body to spirit, leaving more salt here for those who want it. Whole pillars of it.

Lot's wife has no name in the Bible, and if we did not already pick up on it, her presence alone should alert us to the fact God has favorites. Because Lot's wife did nothing egregious. Still she was turned to salt for looking back at Sodom set aflame, because who would not be curious? Former friends and old lovers, charring in an instant. Then killing Lot's wife only punished her daughters.

The Bible and other holy books like to stress salvation, to save one person to others' exclusion. Because these books were written by people, remember. People who like to think better of themselves than others. And they could be right. They could be saved while I am damned, though to this I'm accustomed. A world without my mom already has too little love left in it. So I make salty comment after comment, to the point my husband tells me I've lost my sweetness, for which he married me to begin with. Because I've looked back and watched her dying thousands of times and feel only the need for more water, I don't tell him. Because there are still some ridges within my trachea and I'd like to smoothen them.

Even when I was only eight or nine or ten, I knew I didn't want to live without my mom on this planet, either tomorrow should she die in a car accident or years in the future. The specter of her absence haunted me because she was older and I would likely outlive her, she admitted when I asked. I believed in God too, as she taught me. She told me to pray to him when I really wanted something, and so I prayed for only one thing because I wanted him to concentrate. I prayed for it five or six times a day while still a child and mostly happy. I prayed to die in a car accident—careening off a cliff while flying through the windshield if that were the only way—to die with my mom, whom I wanted with me always.

If that sounds like worship of a woman hardly worth worshipping or something equally strange, I cannot change the reality. Of course, I wanted other things, but she remained so primary I decided I could do without all of life's other good things, including boys I wanted to kiss already, including everything else that would ever happen to me. Including whether I would be homeless and decrepit or go hungry. Including my dad, because I loved him too, but I loved my mom more deeply.

And when I turned twenty, having signed a lease for my first studio apartment, I told her this while she helped me carry a loveseat we'd bought at a used furniture outlet up a stairway. I no longer believed in God, but I wanted her to know this was the only thing I'd ever prayed for seriously. Well you got it, honey, she said smiling. I'm here and I'm healthy.

She loved to drive from southern Indiana to Chicago to visit me, but I have always hated driving. Rather than drive to friends' houses once I turned sixteen, I spent more time painting the bed of the pickup my dad loaned me. The truck had once belonged to his younger brother, who shot himself in the temple one early autumn morning. The truck was blue, and its bed I considered a small ocean, likely because we lived so far from either the Atlantic or Pacific.

I bought paint from the hardware store and brushed yellow shafts of light down its sides in waves suggesting refraction. I painted as many schools of fish as I could in between them, and eventually there were more seahorses than trout or whales or dolphins. I painted each a lighter shade than the one previous, rendering them as a species nearly colorless.

When my mom asked me why I didn't make them brighter, easier to see from a distance, I told her seahorses typically mirror their environment. They camouflage their whole bodies, including prehensile tails they use to clasp eelgrass to avoid being swept away by currents, which can usher them into the maws of predators. Only less than one in a thousand baby seahorses, I told her, survive to adulthood as they drift along the plankton layer of the ocean, borne up by the salt within the water. She said, That's nice, honey, and reverted to weeding our garden.

Barbed Wire Fences

My walls are few, so I have little reason to visit the frame store beside a nail salon in the basement of an apartment complex very often. The salon broadcasts the local news from a television hung above a closet, and I could let someone paint my toenails there if I wanted. I could pay a woman to massage my feet with lotion as I sit smelling fruit from next door that's nearly rotted. The framer leaves orange rinds on the counter by force of habit.

And someday, should the world ever become too lonely a dwelling, I may do this. With the door of the nail salon propped open and its television dilating the latest violence, I could hear the voice of the man who frames my pictures and is soothed by the sound of rain falling onto pavement. When we meet, skies are always drizzling. He inhales from an open window, filling his lungs with petrichor, he tells me.

When I walked inside his shop early last evening for the first time in more than a year, he was listening to the radio, from which the voice of another man yawped, Did you check out her fat ass, bro? I laughed before he saw me, when he turned off the radio and laughed also, until we both decided to pretend neither of us had heard or had asses of our own.

I unrolled a bullfight painted on parchment paper looking like cow hide set to wrinkle in the sun. At first, he selected a frame too light a blonde for the scene's stark palette, though I hoped he would do worse. I hoped there'd be more trial and error than there was. I hoped we'd play with frames for as long as it might take to have my toenails painted one door over. Too quickly, though, I chose a thin black one, which drew the eye to the bullfight set inside the blue matting I'd selected at his suggestion. The frame accentuates the coming massacre, I reflected, when we both laughed, remembering that fat ass as if we both had seen it.

In the seating area of the bullring now hanging in my kitchen, each person looks much the same as the person seated beside him. All their eyes' sclera are bugged toward the bull's horns painted the same whiteness. All are watching the same contest between animal and human. All except a woman in a wedding dress with no groom as a companion, a woman who instead of looking out upon the action is gazing down into her lap where her legs are spread, as if she has a penis tucked inside her folds of fabric.

I want to be this woman, I almost said to the framer when he asked if I wanted glass resisting UV radiation to keep the picture's colors vivid. I too want to watch a bullfight in my wedding dress without a wedding to follow it. This I nearly said to him instead of answering his question, to which I responded yes, let's keep the sun from blinding then erasing her out of existence.

I was wearing neither red nor white when I said this, resembling neither the matador nor the bride in the audience. Instead, I wore a sweater long as a short dress and dyed dark violet. Down its center a braided rope was stitched, dividing my body into eastern and western hemispheres, because my body is its own world and spins on its own axis. An anchor's knot where the equator might have been also tied my heart to my uterus. The knot grew looser when I bent over at the waist and tighter when I arched my spinal column.

The framer asked for my name again, and I told him. Then I left to take a train to the city's outer limits, where I play in an ensemble of Javanese gamelan, a hypnotic Eastern music, though I have never been to Indonesia and doubt I'll ever take the time to visit.

Walking to the train station, I passed a woman selling candles made from beeswax arranged across a table beneath a canvas tent. I stopped and felt the weight of one shaped into a pinecone in my hand and decided it was too heavy to purchase. I also wasn't certain I wanted to brighten my apartment with light stolen from bees, whose hives are places of darkness.

And as the sun began to swell while turning tangerine as it collapsed into the horizon, a man much younger than me asked me for directions, to a restaurant where he was meeting friends. I told him he needed to take the train in the opposite direction I was headed, when he asked if he could walk with me to the station.

I nodded yes, and as we crossed a street, he told me he had moved here recently from Missouri. He had no real job as yet but made ends meet as an exotic dancer on weekends, adding he'd waive his fee for a private performance. I laughed and told him I was married, that he could save his routine for the bachelorettes. Then he rested his hand on the small of my back and let it drop to where my ass began curving, asking me if I minded if he left it there a second. I looked into his face, kept silent. Because the framer and I had found the frame so quickly, hours before the bullfight even started.

A bull kept in a pasture and from all violence exists alone among a herd of females he mounts as he pleases. He fights no other bull to retain his harem and faces no matador in any bullring. Hemmed within a pasture's fences, bulls live longer than most bullfighters on average. Still they are often slaughtered once they become aggressive.

Many farmers favor artificial insemination for this reason, although my dad wasn't among them. Once I witnessed him running from a bull with horns that could have easily impaled him when, recovering his breath after hopping a barbed wire fence and bloodying his hands in the process, he warned me never to climb it. His warning, though, was needless. Like the bride without a husband, I never watched any violence from beyond a safe distance. Looking up from my lap without a penis, I sensed even then I'd do little with my life beyond frame pictures and have my toenails painted.

Walking down the subway stairs to wait on the train, I stepped into water pooling on a stair sunken with too many footsteps. Standing on the platform where more water drained from the ceiling, I became aware of a blackened silence enshrouding the man beside me. Something about him hovering in my peripheral vision suggested he might have been wearing a cape, though when I looked he wasn't. His face turned to meet me, and I saw his eyes were red and filled with liquid, as dirty as the inside of my shoes since I'd stepped into the stairs' depression. He stared into an advertisement for hair dye on the billboard across the tunnel, and I tried to stand as still as he did for a moment. Then the water inside my shoes began to rise and swim, and I started to fidget.

I scraped my heel against a swatch of gum the color of cow tongue, and avoiding the dancer's eyes on the tracks' other side, I stepped onto a train ready to carry me to another basement, where I often suspend my mallets midair. I am sometimes so uncertain of the rhythm I don't play at all through long and longer sections of the song, until it's nearly ended.

Half an hour later, I looked up toward a clock outside a bank and saw I had almost an hour still before my practice started. I shivered and wished I'd brought a jacket now that it was early autumn. Yet soon I'd grow another layer, fatting myself with warmth I carried on my body while staying indoors for longer stretches. Sooner than intended, I'd grow rounder, less visible to exotic dancers.

I walked past a record store and coffee shop shuttered since the summer then inside a tavern where I occasionally order a hamburger and glass of wine for dinner. The bartender smiled at me beneath his beard, and I sat in a booth beneath a light flickering softly as a candle flame. Next weekend was Halloween, and the waitress wore a headband with cat ears as well as a Batman shirt with sequins sewn upon its wings, which expanded like sails over her breasts, as if they were flying. She seemed to be celebrating early, her costume still in the making.

She brought me a carafe of water, and a man brushing past her asked whether she was a cat or a bat. She took her time answering, and I realized the mistake I'd made in not buying the pinecone made of beeswax, in not setting something fallen from the forest aglow in my apartment. The man, I knew, hardly cared if she was a cat or bat or another animal altogether that might wreak more damage. But she was a bat, she said eventually, and left him for the kitchen. She was a bat, and she was awake and flying blindly now that it was evening. Meanwhile I sat staring into my lap as somewhere in southern Spain a matador was taunting a bull this very moment, enraging the animal solely so he has a reason to plunge a sword through a heart easily broken.

Untold images of Jesus in the Catholic religion show him holding his heart outside his body. A crown of thorns pierces its vena cava. To me, though, the thorns always looked more like barbed wire fences, protecting a heart the nuns said was sacred. Yet the fact he so often held it from his chest also indicated he could live without it. At times, Jesus himself was heartless. He could fully function without the organ kept the same as a bull inside his fence, something that should allay any matador's conscience.

In Spain, a room set aside for surgery sits adjacent to every bullring. Alongside the surgeon stands a priest, and on the wall in the infirmary hangs a picture of Jesus holding his heart like an apple he plans on eating. The thorns piercing the fruit symbolize his suffering, and matadors lying prostrate take solace from the image, as if the bull feels nothing.

If a bullfight has a clean finish, the matador stabs the bull fatally in the aorta and the bull dies quickly. But if the matador misses or the heart proves stronger than expected, he attempts to sever the spinal cord with a smaller, second implement. Yet even with its spine chopped all to pieces, the bull still struggles for breath, often for several hours. The matador then hacks away at its vertebrae with a still smaller dagger, until all that remains is a salad of nerves and bone and whatever else had held them together.

The matador's cape is red for only one reason, to camouflage the blood of the bull so the violence doesn't repel the audience. The bull itself is colorblind, however. The blood stains on the cape to the animal being bloodied can also hardly make a difference. Yet if the bride were to step inside the bullring, the bull's blood would loom starkly against her dress's whiteness. The audience would witness the bull more clearly dying by degrees, seeing its life more visibly leaching, the sword thrust in between the fence's openings.

I like to eat alone after visiting the framer, a man I see so seldom he cannot remember my name and I don't expect him to. I like to do a lot of things alone, however. I would gladly watch a matador stab a bull between his shoulder blades in southern Spain, if I could ever convince no one to go with me. I also see no reason to wear a wedding dress unless to stain it red in places. Too much whiteness I reserve for the sides of the eyes only.

After finishing my hamburger and glass of wine and leaving the bar with its bats still ferrying glasses of lager, I left to take a walk before my class, still not for twenty more minutes. I walked past a church then sat in its courtyard beneath a statue of Jesus with his arms outstretched and weighted with marble robes. He looked as if he were pushing against invisible walls beginning to enclose him, as if something he only imagined were the cause of all his suffering. The heart he wore outside his body was ringed in thorns as white as the rest of him while flames were carved shooting out its right atrium.

The thorns—the pain so endless—I understood their symbolism. But the flames, growing from the heart of Jesus as naturally as leaves from a tree in a forest, I didn't. I didn't see where the heat came from within this heart so sacred yet also so white, so exposed to the cool drizzle begun falling. Hunched with my anchor's knot contracted into my abdomen, I was growing too cold to stay here sitting.

If Jesus were a bull, though, one thing is certain. No matador could kill him. Jesus alone can survive holding his heart like an exoskeleton from which he has molted, metamorphosing from mammal into something more reptilian. Yet with Jesus born again and hemmed within a bullpen, the bride must go sooner to her wedding. She can no longer delay it. The bullfight ends too quickly to keep the groom waiting.

When I walked inside the basement and helped to arrange the instruments on the carpet, my teacher asked me if I'd seen the meteor shower this past weekend. I told him I'd missed it. I mentioned the cosmic debris, however, had somehow shattered a vase I'd bought in Turkey shaped into a lotus. The vase had fallen off a bookshelf in the night and shattered into a hundred pieces, I said while folding my legs into a knot, ready to begin playing. His bike light had broken too, he added, making me feel better about so much brokenness. Because few things of value are contained by barbed wire fences. Most go unprotected.

I played poorly all throughout our practice, because I tried a new instrument, which stretched my hand-eye coordination to its limits. My teacher sat across from me, with Javanese spirits hovering between us for five or more minutes, trying to keep me from playing more wrong notes than needed. Eventually I handed him the mallets but scraped his wrist with my fingernail by accident. I scraped him with one of ten I should have cut and painted, if not myself then by someone working beside the framer in the basement. I wanted to apologize but realized it might be better not to acknowledge the cut I'd made where his veins rose closest to the surface. Better to let him hurt in silence.

After stopping the song to play for me by way of demonstration, he asked me to mimic him. I thought I did as well as could be expected, when he smiled and said I gripped the mallets too tightly. Should I let my wrists go limp? I asked him. As if I were lifeless? No, just hold them closer to their ends, as if ready to give them to another person.

I have asked myself, time and again, what makes Jesus' heart so sacred. I have wondered why his heart alone is treated the same as a bull kept by a farmer not practicing artificial insemination. Because Jesus never lusted perhaps. Because he never wanted anyone to untangle his body's prime meridian. Because he was less than human. Because he could survive while holding his heart outside his sternum.

After we finished practicing and were putting away the instruments, I told a woman named Karen I planned on attending an evening of interpretative dance to Java's Dutch colonization, a performance she was curating. While I was saying this, I felt my sleeve begin to itch, a sleeve I'd pushed up to my elbows for freer movement and to too tightly grip my mallet. I had left a tag in place, a sticker reading M for medium inside my wrist, as if it were a secret. My teacher glanced toward my body's axis as I unstuck it while my sweater's knot began to tighten.

As everyone else left the basement to walk outside into the descending autumn, I told my teacher and Karen about the last time I'd visited the space where the Dutch atrocities were being resurrected. I had gone there with my husband to see a puppet show where I had seen no puppets. Instead, I'd witnessed only a woman with mascara smeared across her cheeks take off all her clothes before dissolving into a sheet that nearly suffocated her of oxygen. Her gasping, though, may have been performative. She had not died in the end, only shown us her nakedness.

My teacher said he hadn't known puppetry had gotten pornographic. It's a thing, I told him, as if I were part of it. As if I had seen more than the one instance.

He is a year or two older than myself, 36 or 37, neither of us with any gray hair as yet, only wrinkles ringing our eyes when we smile or laugh. He is the same age as the friend of a friend I haven't seen in years and never liked to begin with, whom I met standing on the corner on my walk back to the train station. She has the ability to stand as still as a bird of prey while I fidget. She saw me before I saw her staring my direction and never blinked all the time we stood talking.

She had called a cab, she said, and was going to her boyfriend's apartment. She added it had been two years or more since we'd last met, while I could not have said. I only noticed half her hair once black was stringed with silver. Otherwise, she looked the same as ever. Not a muscle twitched when a car rolled past with no muffler and nearly killed a cyclist. Then she waved goodbye, saying her taxi was coming, though the street was once more empty.

I walked on past a storefront with bras and matching panties hanging from wire like aerial acrobats. On the window were painted the words, What Is Isn't, which I agreed with, because nothing still made sense, either for the bull or the bride with no penis, for those who lived denied their right to violence. Sense was relegated to those who thrust their swords clean back of the neck and straight toward the bull's aorta for a paycheck. Because no one wants to kill a bull by hacking away at its spinal axis.

The fence surrounding the sacred heart of Jesus is hardly a fence, though, to begin with. It is only a crown of thorns that slid down from his head and now protects an organ slimy as a jellyfish. And killing the bull only saddens the woman wearing a dress too white not to notice, she whose bright red heart beneath it is so sacred she can never hold it. Instead, she sits in a basement waiting for her toenails to be painted. She listens to the news and smells rotting citrus rather than walking to the chapel to pray for her deliverance.

Whip the Bones

This is how she bakes her body into a soufflé. Without access to bowls, eggs, or oven, she crosses her arms into a knot tied with ligaments. She stares at pillows cross-stitched with yellow leaves hardened into lemons. Only the leaves are attacked by butterflies, she can't help but notice. The leaves have no trees while the butterflies are monstrous.

The spread of sunlight staining their wings has rotted symmetrically in places, to look like eyes from a distance—to scare away predators, she realizes—while the leaves spin at pillows' edges. They spin as if the butterflies could do nothing to save them. As if they were not the ones who sent them falling into disintegration.

The butterflies have molted from no pupae yet were born with two sets of eyes nevertheless. Their wings' larger pair has wider pupils to admit no light with which to see no predator walking softly in the forest. Their larvae have never stuck to pillows' surface, have never known the shapelessness of egg whites waiting to be whisked into small, white mountains, into peaks that deflate into craters of albumen. However pretty they may be, she feels slightly sorry for them.

The flapping of their wings is deafening inside Dunkin' Donuts, where she sits drinking coffee with milk curdling into the trunk of an elephant. She stares at her pillows for company, because she has left her keys in another coat pocket while she went shopping for something to soften the arms of her couches. She went looking for these two pillows, it seemed once she saw them, and now she is temporarily homeless. Her husband has also left the apartment and does not answer his phone. Even if he did, he would not return from wherever he has gone, not immediately. He would never understand her urgency to bake a soufflé today rather than wait for tomorrow evening, would hardly register the importance of baking herself with it for flavoring, for sweetness as well as other things. For the pleasure of whipping her bones into cream.

And she must do this quickly. Otherwise, she'll be eaten raw and perhaps poison an innocent person who is hungry. Otherwise, she'll never be prepared and seasoned properly. Rather than being served for a meal's finish, she'll fall victim to birds of prey, which eat anything. Fall victim, she says in a whisper to her own chest cavity, as if being picked apart by birds atop a mountain were a kind of falling, as if this were the same as succumbing to gravity.

She must start by finding a way to beat herself along with however many eggs are listed in the recipe. She must mix them into a froth looking like the crest of a wave lunging toward a quay, one interposed among a row of communist bookstores lining Paris' Left Bank, she's imagining, where she hurtles herself against the Parisian brick with her mouth agape, as if she were the one doing the devouring instead of the cooking. As if she were a wave consuming sand and towels and other dry things. As if the moistness of her body craved an arid settling somewhere she doesn't speak the language yet enjoys the vowels' slurring all the same.

She might begin by flinging herself against the side of a building. She might start by biting her ankles, knotting her skin more tightly, twisting her calves behind her shoulder blades, splintering them for even finer breakage, then turning her feet sideways until they split from the sockets of her legs. Because she must make herself less heavy. There is no bowl inside her kitchen large enough to contain all her veins much less all her arteries. She must start by making herself smaller until she fits inside something.

As it is, she finds her bones so solid she must begin by smashing herself against any available walls while no one is looking. She must fold herself backward again and again until her joints start snapping. At present, however, she feels no pain, because she is only planning the breakage. She folds her legs neatly onto the pink, plastic seat beside which her pillows say nothing. She looks out the window at the beautiful men passing.

And after lunging too far forward trying to see the last of them, she reminds herself she soon will rise over the lip of a ramekin, a ceramic lip she imagines immune from all feeling while her own lips stay parted. As if before baking itself into what amounts to a large French muffin, her body is creating larger openings for air to enter her system. Otherwise, her head will never rise high enough to graze the roof of the oven.

Sky is a relative term, she's decided, while looking up at the blueness behind the clouds' shattering white. And she will settle for a gray one. She must, because the oven is aluminum.

Were she only living in Tibet instead of Midwestern America, were she only Buddhist instead of nothing, she could deploy a rogyapa, or breaker of bodies, to chop her bones into smaller pieces while she still breathes, leaving her lungs intact for whatever may qualify as the time being. She could summon a man to detach her hair from the scalp beneath with a knife sharpened for the ritual flaying. She could instruct him to break her joints and sever her limbs from her torso the same as he does with those monks who have outlived their dotage, those who keep dying yet may escape further reincarnating, those who may transcend samsara while she keeps being born in different bodies. Almost daily, he separates meat from bone, spreading out the fat of inner thighs among stones silent with knowledge. He is giving the birds their alms, because she has stolen the air from them all along without knowing.

As it is, she feels more French than Tibetan, if only because she has been to France while she grows dizzy at high altitudes, it seems, so dizzy that while traveling in the Peruvian Andes she retched all her dinner into a toilet each evening. She also doesn't like climbing, mountains least of all. She prefers baguettes, scarves, and riding bicycles through gardens on flat topography. She prefers French accents and the love they make in movies.

The donuts lining the shelves to her left would sicken any Parisian, she thinks. The donuts would force a populace known for being snobbish to turn their lean violin noses up toward the ceiling without playing any music. And she feels herself superior thinking of the soufflé she plans on baking, superior to the man behind the counter selling donuts filled with jelly as well as superior to the Tibetan Buddhists busy breaking bodies. She will boil her blood into a reduction. For a sauce, she thinks.

She has spent only a few weeks in Paris, a little less in Provence and the Cote d'Azur, where people sunbathe naked in public. Still this was long enough for her to understand that despite being from Indiana, despite eating corn on the cob all four seasons because some was always kept frozen, she is French by disposition. She is French by virtue of liking to eat and taking her time about it, by luxuriating in wiping her chin with a napkin and doing nothing for the remainder of the evening. She is French enough to bake a soufflé with a woman inside it.

Everything happens for a reason, people are fond of saying. The reason she fell from out her mother's body, she's now prepared to counter if anyone raises the subject, is to rise with the yeast. She knows few facts, but this has made itself apparent. She is too succulent not to make use of the juices that leach from each orifice.

She walks to the unisex bathroom as if entering a chateau in Brittany, where she bends her head to lick the sweat pooling in her elbow crease. She runs a finger between her legs then lifts each breast to moisten the shadow space. She extends her tongue and gives herself a taste.

Only until she can leave Dunkin' Donuts without freezing on her doorstep, she cannot begin baking. She half feels she's being delayed on purpose, though she tries not to resent it. She remembers that human bodies once warm to aching are being devoured by birds in the Himalayas. She takes

178

cold comfort in it.

Yet rather than snacking on herself amid anodyne graffiti on a public toilet, she would like to feel the cut of a spoon through her skin. She would like to experience herself being eaten, to shiver at the spoon's steel ablation through her organs. She would like to sense someone else's tongue come alive with the taste of her, someone who will let her linger. He'll hold her there a second while she swings on his uvula until she becomes quiet, until she falls down his trachea with a cascade of saliva.

She washes her hands and returns to her pillows. She imagines herself being swallowed as her head collapses onto the table in the nest of her elbow. She transfers her heat to its surface, not quite liking to share the warmth of her body with something inanimate, something with no gustatory sensation, no mouth to taste with.

Her mom used to wish she'd become a journalist, a vocation that would have made use of her bent for talking ad nauseum, for lapsing into prolix description. Only she never cared for facts, still doesn't. To facts, she has always preferred eating. What little news she bothers reading strikes her as doggerel absent all comedy, as metaphor for appetite alone. The only thing she knows for certain is that we are hungry.

Spirits are even hungrier evidently, though about them journalists write next to nothing. Tibetans believe traditionally that vultures are more than the scavengers they seem. They imagine the birds as dakini, female goddesses inhabiting the upper regions of the atmosphere who fly without feathers, who are held aloft by only their desire for men with the phalluses of gods presumably. And bird goddesses of the Paleolithic Period suit her sensibilities, especially if they grow angry on occasion and start pecking at those still living. Especially if the arches of their eyebrows are lined with electricity.

The earliest known cave paintings are found in southern France, a place where people appreciate a souffle's airy beauty. At Pech Merle in the Midi-Pyrénées, pregnant bird women dance on a cave ceiling. Some anthropologists suggest these are female shamans of primordial Asian cultures from the Silk Road dating back to the Iron Age, when the world began teeming with weaponry. She reflects on this while still stirring the milk inside her coffee, dissolving the elephant's trunk into an elephant body. The only way to grow wings, she reflects, as a woman these days is to feed yourself to the dakini, to sacrifice your body so they can digest your entrails then fly for longer and scavenge at a wider ambit. To become part of them while being yourself no longer.

The lightest she has felt within memory, the closest she has ever come to being a soufflé still rising, was when being pushed on a wooden swing her dad had made and hung from a tree. Yet she can no longer replicate this feeling without baking her body, without subjecting herself to a terrible heat incinerating her outermost layer. Only when your leavening deflates too quickly, no one considers you a fact worth reporting.

The only person who may appreciate the wisdom of her decision is her handyman, David, the only person who might be in possession of fewer facts than she is. He is installing new blinds in her apartment and has left his drill on the windowsill in her kitchen for days now on end. He started divorce proceedings a few months before this, but his wife has since returned with their old curtains. They are trying to get along again.

David smiles and talks to her as if she were a friend when she isn't. He has no sense of the wind blowing through her from all the emptiness she's known inside her apartment the same size as his. He may eat all her bones regardless, because her husband doesn't like chocolate, and this is the kind of soufflé she will be. It has been decided.

She calls him eventually around 4:30 p.m. even though he's told her and all the other tenants never to call him on weekends. He once posted a sign about it in the building's entrance. Only she's already spent three hours at Dunkin' Donuts drinking one cup of coffee and is growing restive. He is driving back into the city, though, from Michigan, he tells her when she calls him. And he's sorry he can't help. He really is.

She sits for a few more minutes then walks down the street and starts pressing buttons, all the buzzers lining the entrance. She presses them as if they're a control panel for a spaceship and all the other astronauts' heads have exploded from forgetting to wear their helmets when sticking their heads out for less oxygen. And now it's up to her to steer the vessel back to her home planet. Because limitless as the universe seems from this vantage, there's only one place she knows of that allows her the pleasure of eating pastries on summer grasses. There's only one planet with a Paris. Someone eventually buzzes her in, when she sits on the stairs outside the three rooms she and her husband rent for too much money. Most of her neighbors are watching television. She listens carefully for fucking but can't hear any.

And while she waits on the stairwell crusted with dead ants, she imagines this as a lustrum, the interval of rest between two censuses when Rome was ancient. She imagines someone a floor above or below her is offering the gods a sacrificial lamb, because gods like mutton, or they did according to early Romans. She imagines they'll want a light dessert to complement it, a soufflé lighter than a soufflé has ever been, a soufflé almost too human, rising and falling as if breathing and containing its own contradictions. One that seems to hesitate, unsure of being eaten.

She has never seen much of a reason for counting, because in time the total will only change again. So a lustrum to her makes more sense than a census, though if you have an empire, you want to know how much of it there is, she acknowledges. If you have nothing, you resign yourself to a period of restfulness. You resign yourself to waiting the day's remainder on your husband to let you into your apartment, where you have nothing in particular to do but can at least finger yourself in private.

Once he comes home an hour or so later and finds her slumped on the stairs, she walks to the kitchen in silence. She opens her cupboard and confronts her bowls stacked one within the other, and part of her questions the value of whipping her bones inside them. Part of her prefers simply standing here in their presence.

In recent days, she has lost all her writing work that pays anything while several friends have moved to different cities. She has no one now except her husband she can talk to in the evenings. The music classes she has been taking have also been canceled, because only one other person felt they were vital to keep living. So she sits home on weekdays and does nothing except listen whole hours to the parrots across the hall, because David rescues them from bird adoption agencies. Because although they could easily spend their days relaxing, the parrots are panicked. They tweeze out their feathers with their beaks when they might be resting.

Yet while the parrots are crying, she feels her body loosen. She feels her tendons melt like icing across a cake just risen with no intent of collapsing. Because there is less of her since the emptiness inside her has expanded with her life now filled by next to nothing, there is also less to mix with the flour and eggs once she starts cooking. And the less time spent mixing, the sooner the feast begins. For the moment, however, she's not hungry.

Still she turns on the oven then feels her elbows soften. Her bones will break more easily if she coaxes them with heat. She knows this instinctively despite the fact this is her first time cooking anything living. She feels herself dissolving and loving the feeling. For the feeling to continue, she will do what is necessary.

She is not unhappy. She only finds herself in the process of being emptied to yield more easily to leavening. There is nothing in her life now to keep her from devolving into anomie. Yet instead of this, instead of sleeping late or drinking, she has begun smelling things. A few days before this, she left two wool sweaters at the dry cleaners, sweaters she had dirtied and did not want to shrink. She left the sweaters then lingered. The owner was ironing a pair of trousers, and the smell of the steam was intoxicating.

Water become steam, the smell of heat escaping, is now to her a body. It is the only species of lover she expects to meet in an afterlife she has already begun anticipating. She feels the vapors kneading her shoulder blades, and because she has so little to occupy her time these days, she feels a presence even from an iron exhaling. She now needs almost nothing, as she too is becoming vaporous. She now is only witness to everything else happening. She knows no facts and does no counting. She has never baked a soufflé before this and is also out of eggs, which she has no intention of buying.

All she knows of soufflés, none of which she can now remember eating, is that they collapse shortly after they're done cooking. They collapse within themselves five to ten minutes after being taken from the oven. The meringue cannot sustain its own lightness and quickly deflates, often rupturing. Resourceful cooks fill the cracks with sauce or cream so its insides seem to be bleeding.

She is not resourceful, however. She cooks next to nothing and eats out most evenings. She has the time to cook but none of the equipment. No ramekins, no spatula, no whisk. No eggs, flour, or sugar either, because she pours only milk in her coffee. She has only an empty bowl and her own body, which over the years she's fattened to make the whipping easier.

Yet she has felt less hungry than normal lately, which is odd for someone who regards food with a French woman's sensuality. She feels as if all her organs have been whipped together in her sleep, until soft foam peaks have begun to form from her kidneys. She feels them poking through her when she wakes. It is a pleasure poking.

She feels so much less solid of late that sometimes she suspects she is being prepared rather than doing the preparing. She feels she is being made ready by simply being willing, to the point she wonders whether she invoked all this emptiness subconsciously, whether she caused the work and friends and music classes all to vanish. She half suspects she has done it by some secret wishing, has desired the nothing into being. Because what else explains the sudden love of steam released from the pores of an iron? Something she formerly would have never noticed. She sits peacefully for hours and watches her pillows' yellow leaves falling.

Fifteen years before this, her mom gave her a bottle of lotion, a plastic container shaped like a ramekin. A body soufflé, it said on the package. A body soufflé made from no body, there was hardly any need to explain. She didn't open it until yesterday, when she rubbed some around her navel then smoothed it down her legs.

The lotion looked yellowed with age, though it may have been yellow to begin with. Once she opened it, she couldn't resist patting it, as if it were the face of a child or the rump of a kitten. It was a soufflé never fallen, and even when her mom gave it to her, she wanted to preserve it always. She wanted to pack then carry it from one apartment to the next. Up until this point, she has done this.

And as she sat listening to the parrots—wondering about their squawks' significance, what past trauma still haunted them—she smelled something pleasant, something richer than steam. It was the soufflé she'd spread on her body earlier that morning. The fragrance suffused not only her skin but her whole empty existence. Had her life been more crowded, she would not have smelled this. She wondered why she waited so long to open it.

Perhaps she didn't need to bake anything, she then reflected. Perhaps

184

she was already cooking. She was becoming lighter already, browning from the sunlight filtering through windows shaded only by trees still leafless. Possibly her mom was baking her, keeping busy in the kitchen her daughter hardly uses. Her mom was doing the cooking while leaving her to leisure. Such is the benevolence of female spirits.

Her body soufflé is scented with vanilla and lavender. These words are still legible beneath the cap, though the list of ingredients has worn away. Fifteen years and still the soufflé feels springy. The lotion is just as buoyant when she slaps it as it would have been if she had opened it years before this. Though for this she knows there is only one reason. Because she has always walked softly in her socks while a cake cooks in the oven. Her mom never made a soufflé to her knowledge, but she made cakes fairly often, and the principle is the same. To whisper and tiptoe around them.

She knows she could consider herself done baking if she wanted. She could sit here doing nothing beyond smelling the lavender and vanilla baked into her skin, because the heat in her apartment makes the air feel tropical while the snow is falling. She could sit here admiring her own body, her thumbs particularly. Because they stick off her hand sideways as if they want to say something, though they never speak. Below them, her wrists have lines ringed around them. As if she has done nothing with her life but bend them.

Metal bends because of certain crystal patterns. It is miraculous according to the man who wrote a new book about it, a book of which she read only the dust jacket. Still it is a fact. It is a hunger for something. We want metal to curve and so we heat then reshape it, into a clothes hanger perhaps. Whereas her thumb curves out from her wrist without being asked, though this is not a fact. It is a beauty she can witness.

Sometimes she wonders whether all this heat inside her—she feels it, she feels it each day more strongly—will ever cool, whether she will ever stop being this oven baking her innards. She is a young woman no longer, yet still the heat rises inside her as if she's not done cooking. The heat rises as if trying to alchemize something, as if it wants her to keep taking off her clothes, exposing the crack of her buttocks to men as she's walking.

This while her apartment's oven isn't even working. Next morning David comes over, apologizing again that he couldn't let her in when he was driving back from Michigan. He wrests the oven from the wall after wiping the sweat from his face with his collar. He mends the appliance and smokes a cigarette on the fire escape.

From the other side of the kitchen window, which now is open, he says she should turn down the heat, that this place is steaming. Her skin meanwhile starts to pickle, as if pickles ever solve anything, and he mentions she has done a nice job decorating. When he comes back in, she shows him the terrarium she's filled with red mosses, which the florist told her formed from two other types of mosses mating. Two green ones make a ruddy baby, but David has little interest in plants this pretty. His eyes shift from the terrarium to the chess board she has resting on a drum, neither of which she plays. He tells her to come see his apartment, what he's done with a place that's the mirror image.

Only his wife is sleeping. She'll have to walk as if a cake is baking and take off her shoes. And once she does this, once she pads inside behind him, in his eyes she sees a knowing. She sees his eyes follow hers around his living room, grazing the lamp with a lion head for a base with zebra stripes crisscrossing its shade, so the torso of one animal rests on the head of another species. She compliments him on the silver wallpaper that looks made from fogged mirrors from a distance when she catches the light reflecting off a steel pole beside a clock face. That's Kara's, for practicing, he says as if she's asked him a question when she hasn't. Kara is a stripper, she realizes. She regularly hears someone come in at 5:30 in the morning.

She turns her attention to the curtains, patterned with the blue chains of chain-linked fences, keeping the room in darkness, cooler as he likes it. Were his curtains open, she could nearly see the building where she lived ten years before this, in a studio apartment. She has not come far, she realizes, and this is evidence. To save money then, she heated her little room with her oven, which her mom thought hilarious but her boyfriend, now her husband, said was dangerous. Why? she asked him. Because the gas could clot her lungs with carbon monoxide and she could die from the poison. Only how would she know and what would be the harm? she asked. Because she would be sleeping, she continued, silent. She would be cooking herself without knowing it. She would be dreaming while draining her blood of oxygen.

This would be the way to leave this world, she still thinks, in a peaceful somnolence, the warmest of escape routes to becoming a dakini. Only now her husband pays for heat while she pays for Internet access; they divide utilities. Still she wants to make her oven useful, cooking more than ordinary things.

If no rogyapa will break her for faster feeding to the vultures, she will still make herself lighter. She will sneak back into David's apartment and let the parrots peck at her. She will let them devour the meat between her ribs, the softest parts of the body, which the *Tibetan Book of the Dead* maintains is illusion. She will allow them this rather than continuing to pluck out their own feathers, allaying their sense of abandonment when they've been adopted.

Leaving David, she walks back to her own apartment, where there is no pole beside the mantle, and takes off all her clothes. She does this knowing all cadavers buried in the sky by Buddhists are exposed equally to the elements. The bodies are all naked, and there is no embalming as there is no need of preserving that which is lifeless. Although she has cut herself by accident so often when slicing onions and shaving her legs in the shower, her skin feels unbroken.

She tells herself this is decadence, this undressing before a window so closely facing another across the courtyard and out of which someone might be looking. The sun's glare prevents her from seeing in, though no one is likely home because this is late Monday morning. She tells herself this is the reverse of being sexless while, in the absence even of eyes only staining the wings of butterflies that are not cross-stitched, she undresses for the bird women alone, she realizes.

Revealing of skin she knows too is not enough. Still she hates to think that, were she only Tibetan, someone would break her spine for her, severing it in several places so she could be carried more easily up the mountain and be done with it. She hates the ease she cannot access. The vultures will never find her laid upon stones scented with juniper to attract their notice. Because however lovely the splay of bones upon a mountain, the rogyapa would mix her bone dust with barley flower for easier digestion.

And while she heats herself into something lighter, there is no one to see her, no one to put money in her panties as they would those of Kara. Hers are white cotton with red stitching looking like tiny firework explosions. Before David fixed the oven, he repaired the bedroom blinds, because they were falling without her having noticed and her husband had called him without her knowledge. Their hamper was propped against the window, and so many of her panties are stained with the remnants of menstruation, stained brown as if returned to their real color, drained of their faded fireworks. Because this is what happens once blood reaches the dryer. The lining of her uterus resembles mud being splattered. Five pairs of them sat on top of her husband's shirts, looking spotless in comparison.

And David must have seen them. He may have even smelled them, because she imagines this is not beyond him. He must have wondered why she keeps them. He says he cleans his floors every morning, says he cannot leave a dirty dish in the sink, so this may disgust him. A woman wearing underwear that is clean but looks damaged by fluids detergent won't reverse into whiteness. She doesn't bother bleaching them because her husband doesn't notice.

Ten years ago she and her husband, whom she then was only dating, were watching Olympic ice skating in her studio apartment around the corner. They were lying on her bed when she leapt up and started twirling. I'm doing a triple axel! I'm triple axeling! she started shouting then laughing once she felt dizzy. She spun herself so fast, so deliriously, she lost her balance and fell against the window frame. The window fell out onto a parking space. She then fell partially with what quickly crashed to pieces, when she surrendered to the falling. She felt the end of her life approaching, and her husband not yet her husband didn't try to save her, at which they both laughed once she recovered—once she somehow fell forward, hysterically laughing. Her heart was pounding through her chest loudly as a hammer striking something harder. And yet it had been glorious, the almost dying. The twirl so thrilling her carpet became as slippery as ice in the Olympics.

The March ice on the sidewalk has started melting. The temperature has begun shifting so quickly she now wears layers she can take off easily when she grows warm, when she can pretend someone is watching when he isn't. She can pretend someone is sitting at his kitchen across from her bedroom window not eating anything, only holding out his fork pretending it can be used for tuning, that it resonates at a pitch she'd recognize as perfect had she better hearing, if only it struck something.

Even people with no thoughts of baking their body are attuned to a beautiful body approaching. Even forks vibrate to a certain kind of music, to heartbeats, to the sound of quiet breathing as well as other things. And while she molts out of her sweaters and jeans, she remembers that sky burial is only a matter of convenience for those who live in certain climates, those born closer to the heavens than she will ever see. Tibetan monks living closer to rivers bury their dead subaqueously, though several traditions maintain that water burial is for beggars only, because compared to mountains, rivers are lowly. As if beggars were so uncommon, as if none of us have ever asked for anything. Pleaded over and over more likely. As if beggars too should not be fed to the bird women, about whom they may have fantasized in their poverty.

At the moment there is too much of her, she realizes, to fit inside an oven. Her bones are too strong for her, though they will shrink in time. But it is good, she tells herself while smelling her wrists perfumed with juniper essence, and she begins to dance as if on ice across her kitchen. It is good. It is holy. To be eaten. She says this over and over.

Rice Paddy Hips

In itself it is nothing, a meeting place of the upper and lower eyelids. Medical dictionaries define the canthus as an angle, and inside those either side of the nose's bridge is wedged a seed, as I've long thought of it, a pink globule housing tear ducts as well as other fluids. Science terms it the lacrimal caruncle, yet it remains a pink seed regardless, one containing who knows how many emotions distilled into liquid. One best left to rot inside the head and never planted.

I was walking beside my husband after leaving a puppet museum in Lisbon when I scratched at my eye, clawing the seed by accident. With what had begun to redden, I looked down at my hands, at their veins' river deltas rising closer to the surface. I felt soothed by the currents as my eye filled with liquid. All this water swimming beneath my skin. I had almost forgotten.

Puppets in Vietnam walk on water the same as Jesus, though no one there thinks them miraculous. In Lisbon's Museu da Marioneta, I watched several puppets of Vietnamese origin circulate through a pool filtered by a fountain. I read that when farmers flood their rice fields to increase production, puppet theatres traditionally entertain the children. Rice paddies act as makeshift stages while water flows beneath puppets that take no notice, that themselves are wooden. Whereas were no water flowing through our systems, we too would grow stiff. Our hips would lose their roundness. Women in particular would look misshapen.

Seen either in photographs or from a distance, rice paddies bewitch with their curvature while enfolding mountains in a reflective lushness. The fields themselves resemble female hips, I realized in Lisbon. One hip looks layered upon another as if resting in some small bed together, and I like the look of rice paddies built in terraces better than mountains if I'm honest. The

191

former look softer, more natural even, if manually constructed.

If you watch videos of Vietnamese puppet theatre or manage to see a performance in person, you'll notice no speech accompanies the drama. No narrator explains the surge of flood waters either to the puppets or the children. Likewise, no one ever bothers asking where the deluge comes from, whether fallen from the sky or flowing out the veins of those who carved the puppets. Silence, though, is its own body of water. The deeper, the more life stirring at its bottom.

Were I a child in rural Vietnam, were a child there and I to somehow change places, I too would await the puppets' silence once the rains started. As it is, I sit in my apartment watching my table grow waves across its surface. I sit and extend my hands out toward its surface. I half pretend the table and I are a body connected, Siamese twins bearing each other no resemblance. My table, though, has forgotten how to be flat. It wants to play osmosis.

Only it has done even more than this, more than become a watery island. My table has also become convinced it's a cloud in the process of formation, water being evaporated. Having fallen too many times asleep with visions of casting shadows over oceans, it has decided these waves it has sprouted are only symptomatic of the process, that desire something to happen and that's all there is to it. To me, this is only further confirmation the table is a woman, something hard being melted into liquid. Still I have my doubts whether it can ever become vaporous, because every transformation has its limits.

Yet my table imagines—it daydreams, it fantasizes—clouds have someone always touching them, fingers continually reshaping their edges. Instead of shape shifters, it thinks of clouds as more akin to shapes being shifted, their corners constantly smoothened to look like this or that animal or body part of a human before attenuating into something formless, an airborne protozoan. The touching, it thinks, in the sky is endless. Otherwise, it has no

192

way to account for all its changes.

This prospect of touch that never ceases has become my table's obsession, and I consider myself to blame for this, if only because I never caress its varnish. All I do is bump my shins against its corners then scream at it. Whether the table is a cloud more solid than average, that it is tired of holding things, mostly my cups of coffee, is definite.

Instead of lavishing it with the attention that is clearly needed, I sit mostly in the armchair opposite. I sit and read and ignore it while pulling my skirt up over my hips. I do this only so I can enjoy the crude curve of where my femur fits inside my socket, where the flesh covers over it and leaves a slight sulcus. Unlike the legs of my table, which stand always stiff, mine are easily bended.

If the table could only do this, growing waves then evaporating them into cloud formations might seem less important. With its own woman hips, it might simply walk back and forth across the kitchen then call it quits. As it is, of the two of us only I can feel the soft sweep of mine whenever I wish. It is likely for this reason I'm in no hurry myself to be shape shifted.

Luigi Galvini famously brought the thigh muscles of a frog back from the dead by touching them with a scalpel live with electric current. He had manifested the life force latent within all matter, he felt certain. His nephew later did the same with a human corpse hanged in a London prison, where the muscle contortions thrilled the audience. The prisoner, though, soon fell dead again back inside his coffin.

And I have tried to tell my table it might want to reconsider its cloud aspirations. It might want to revisit metamorphosing into something that will only resemble something else, a frog or an ostrich for instance, and that for only a few seconds. I have at times even lost my patience with it becoming liquid. I've told it that while its waves are lovely for the moment, if I ever decide to rest my feet on it—if I drop a curling iron or toaster on it by accident—I'll be electrocuted. I have reminded it that dead thighs twitch only when connected to an electric outlet, because electricity can kill you as well as seem to set your body in motion. Because all these changes, from lifelessness to back again, are no answer to loneliness. I have no other table, however, for it to make friends with.

I once knew a man, an engineer at a museum where I worked in the cafe, who lived in a high rise stacked beside several others like it. He said each night around eleven a woman in the opposite building vacuumed naked. Every man in his apartment complex knew about it, and summer evenings they gathered on the roof to watch her clean. There were other acts, he mentioned—some women played with their clitoris, some merely stripped— though he always liked the vacuumer best for a reason he didn't bother explaining.

And though I've never seen any of them and am far more interested in men—of crashing into them, as if waves were rolling on my skin's own surface—I have decided she is also my favorite, because she dared to dabble with emptiness. Because the vacuum was probably never plugged in, I imagine she didn't try to make it into something it wasn't. She likely didn't try to fill the vacuum, good woman, with any lint. I also doubt she did this without having pretty hips. Because she could have covered them with an apron if she wanted.

Mine are so lovely sometimes I wonder what to do with them. I briefly considered taking a class in miming—considered then decided against it—if only to watch my hips swivel around my waist in a larger mirror than I have in my apartment. I considered this until I remembered mimes' black and whiteness, their refusal to wear any other colors, either of blood flowing to the heart bright and scarlet or filling veins' river deltas.

Wanting to stare for hours at your own hips is also a poor reason for whitening your face then painting false eyebrows above those you were given, for looking more surprised than you are or ever have been. For this, I could simply stand and look in the bathroom mirror if I wanted, though my face is not as nice as my hips to look at, though my mirror ends at my ribs' bottom. My bathroom is also so small I can hardly turn around inside it, and this is my hips' main attraction. Their capacity for movement. Their wide and free ellipse, the orbit that looks lopsided until it isn't.

I also don't want to pretend I'm climbing a rope or fleeing a bear and running into a tree, for instance, inflicting feigned violence on myself that may end up doing real damage. I don't want to pretend to be someone other than I am, pretending I am someone who always stays silent, someone who cannot speak to the audience if she feels like it. Instead of miming, I've simply started sliding my hands up and down my hips in private, for no one else to witness. At times, though, I do forget they exist. At times, I do just walk with them. Only once I remember them again do I feel I have left them friendless. I become keenly aware of their loneliness. Because just as my table's waves might become clouds at any moment, clouds either shape shifting or shape shifted, I might also wake and find myself turned wooden. These round hips might become square edges. In time, I might become a table myself holding cups and vases. As you grow older, you must expect some changes.

I didn't notice the waves rising from my table until I came home from Lisbon and scratched my canthus. Yet ever since, I can feel how many cups my table is holding, how many have gone unwashed since the previous evening as I brush my teeth a room away in the morning. I have become more sensitive to liquid flowing within a solid-seeming body, to how long I have until my table hangs vaporous above me, until it floods the fields and brings forth the puppets.

And as the table lightens while undulating with waves, I can hear music.

Off the coast of the Adriatic Sea in some small Croatian village, tides force air through a series of tubes built into revetments, mimicking the sound of a pipe organ. In Chicago where I live with my table and husband, city planners are likewise in the process of building one similar to it around a shoal overlooking a shipwreck long sunken in Lake Michigan. Each summer, thousands of people swim out to sunbathe on the ship's surface. Divers rest on the rusted boiler where seagulls also perch, finding it convenient.

The Silver Spray ran afoul of too large of waves a century before this, though most of the passengers stayed aboard because a stew was cooking, the newspapers later reported. The cook had just finished setting the table when the storm split into a reckoning. The ship, for the record, was also a woman. Women, though, may be swatted to pieces and still hear a melody floating through their wreckage. The world grows quiet only once rain falls from clouds onto rice paddies.

If this table ever does vaporize into what I will never recognize again, because clouds change too quickly, that will also be the end of me with it. Because I too must have my transformation, because I would no longer be a woman, and that is all I have ever known of this body. No longer feeding stew to hungry men well on their way to dying, with no more hips resembling Vietnamese rice paddies, I'll turn yet more to liquid once my veins' river deltas flow toward their ocean. I'll melt entirely before I become wooden.

And a woman must have waves rounding her hips so she can pretend to vacuum naked for the men in the apartment building opposite. She must seem to clean the carpet while keeping the vacuum a container of only emptiness. Seeming to sing in silence, she is a mime with no makeup except for some red lipstick.

There are no safe landings in a human body. This alone do I see clearly. Because although my vision is unchanged since going to Lisbon, the seed inside me now knows it must succumb to flooding. It will be drowned along with everything else inside me.

This drowning, I try to tell myself, is a beginning. Drowning brings forth the puppets, which glide smoothly over water's surface. Lacquered so they can scratch their faces without scarring their cheeks, they appear only once the rice has been planted. Without any vision to begin with, they cannot be blinded. They walk on water before every harvest.

Healing Waters

A tornado's intake of breath uprooted a pine tree in my parents' garden. Early on a Sunday morning, my mom calls and tells me this. She asks me what they would have done if it had hit the house while they were sleeping. For several moments, I stay silent. I play with the satin ties of my pajamas as I allow something mute yet becoming solid to expand between us. I allow this rather than anything else I might have spoken to express my relief at being better protected from the elements.

Had the tornado flicked its tail toward the kitchen, they would have been flattened, I eventually say in response. I say this aware I can afford to be callous, if only because my parents have escaped the damage. I am also in the process of distancing myself from their goodness, too much of which and even natural phenomena can take advantage.

A family living half a mile away lost their home and one of their children, my mom takes a deep breath and mentions. A girl of nine or ten was struck fatally by a fence post, her heart's electricity darkened by nothing more than air turned into something almost human, into wind tilting its head down toward its sternum. Lumber, siding, and insulation have splayed themselves across fields of autumn soybeans.

My parents lose power for days on end. They survive on canned tuna and boxes of raisins in the wake of the tornado's county-wide destruction. Meanwhile I order Thai in and refuse to come any closer to the wind spinning itself around them. I could live within easier driving distance, nearer the eye of a storm where all the world goes quiet. I could take the Greyhound down to visit them more often. Instead, I sign a new lease on a studio apartment a few blocks away from a train that sounds like but never is a tornado approaching in the distance.

After her talk of death and near death is finished, my mom asks if I'll take three days off in January to go skiing with the two of them and my younger sister, soon home for winter break from her freshman year of college. My mom has two weeks off for the holidays from her job as a school counselor, and my dad can pay someone else to feed his heifers. They have not taken a vacation in four years, she tells me. She has never seen the Rockies.

There will be hot springs too, she whispers once I agree. Healing waters, she suspires into the phone's speaker. She says we can all cure ourselves of our maladies in Steamboat Springs, where there are never any steamboats wheeling down any rivers, only mountains made steeper by the rain's dull carving. In this northern Colorado town my mom has read about in a magazine, tornadoes are not a danger. Air does nothing except flush skiers' faces, leaving them free to widen the angle of their skis when they feel afraid of flying.

I was 22, five months out of college, and working at a translation company a floor below the headquarters of *Playboy* magazine when my mom booked our flight to Steamboat Springs. Hired as a project manager, I translated nothing, only arranged for others to convert tracts of Tagalog or Urdu into English and then sent them payment. Two months after I returned from what was our final family vacation without our knowing, I was fired for overpaying some translators and underpaying others at random. Something about my presence had also thickened the air in the office, my boss mentioned. I'd declined chances to represent our company at conventions and left co-workers' birthday parties early, she remembered. I'd worked mostly wordlessly, spending my lunch hours reading. Between chapters, I wondered what I'd sacrificed for the city's sirens, for its seeming safety.

On the ground floor of our office building was a market where I often bought lunch from the deli. Over the past few months, I'd fallen a little in love with the man who worked the counter and he a little in love with me,

I felt without knowing. Once he grew used to seeing my face a couple times a week, he started casually interrogating me, when I told him I was dating someone, had moved here for college from rural Indiana, and didn't work for *Playboy* magazine.

With his blue eyes shining, he once asked me whether our farm had animals, when I nodded, asking for more mayonnaise. He asked what kind—any goats or sheep?—and when I told him pastel ponies with rumps embossed with cupcakes, he laughed until I felt afraid he'd slice a finger off as he shaved a ham shank. In response, I only looked at him saying, What, you don't believe me?

I wasn't lying either entirely. As a little girl, I'd sent several of my plastic ponies swimming down an emerald creek cleaving our south pasture into what I always thought of as two separate countries. Letting go of tails I'd finished braiding, I felt sure I'd lose them even if they didn't sink, because my ponies had no muscles to tense against the currents that knocked them sideways. They could never step with their little lavender legs back onto the bank, so I knew I as good as killed them in the swimming. The creek also ran only in one direction, as do most things. It widened toward a river running toward an ocean I had never seen.

To my mom, I pretended the ponies had simply fallen, and in her goodness she believed me. Together we mourned their drowning as I imagined they were victims of the creek's torrents versus my hand's weaker hold on things. I pretended this while letting one pony after another tumble down the jaundiced grass blades.

I have no real explanation for why I did this except that some part of me must have been practicing. Forcing my ponies to suffer, to surrender to annihilation for me, I was trying to be braver than my parents, for whom death—of cows, of Jesus Christ on Good Friday, of their own parents, of the prospect of my little sister's disappearance once when she went missing—was all tragedy. At each fresh instance of life succumbing to undoing, their eyes reddened, revealing cracks concealed within the whiteness. Little girl that I was, I felt stronger than them already.

After being fired from my job at the translation company, I left without saying goodbye to the man in the deli. Occasionally, my life still seems loveless enough for me to wonder if he and others like him, those grown familiar though known only in passing, have ever missed me. I wonder only because these kinds of love, given freely with exchange of first names only, still often mean more than necessary. Likely, they loom larger for all that has gone missing.

Rain does not drain passively down the Rockies. Anyone who has ever fallen, though, knows this. Anyone who has ever fallen knows that falling requires your consciousness. As rain collapses down a mountain, each droplet likewise grows rounder at its bottom. Each small liquid island absorbs minerals from rock it scrapes before resting in a cavern. Yet even here, even fallen, water undergoes further transformation. It expands into steam under pressure from lava heating the base of the mountain. Steam in turn escapes from a hot spring in the shape of tongues long and lisping, tongues later summoning a crepuscular flood of human bodies. Late into the evening, men and women float naked in water so warm they mistake it for healing.

Our first morning in Colorado, we walked past a man holding a falcon outside a bakery. He wore a fleece jacket over armor fitted to musculature that may or may not have filled its cavities. In a bucket at his feet, a rock halfway turned to crystal and gently luminescing weighted bills crusted with snow. I half suspected the rock of being more alive than the man or his falcon, because neither moved nor blinked. If we drop some change in the bucket, maybe one will come to life, I offered to my parents by way of asking them for money I'd forgotten to bring. That I would toss it away so easily, they said, was what came of me living in a city.

My mom shivered as we left the bakery, saying birds with such long talons gave her the willies. She didn't understand why anyone would want to train a predator species, and my dad agreed. I could see some, though, I offered, if only because raptors do not land willingly on a human body. Once a falcon slays its prey, the falconer hides the carcass, keeping the bird hungry enough to keep stalking. And I could take some satisfaction from harnessing a power so instinctive, I added with them no longer caring. I thought I could learn to take pleasure in the weight of something deadly resting on my shoulder.

I had no reason to suspect my parents were both dying then from different forms of cancer. Still something inside me resisted their aversion to power that lay beyond them, the power even of nature's destruction, which I would have to contend with far longer. I defended falconry fully aware that, free from human intervention, the falcon could have guarded better against starvation, eating all the quarry it wanted.

That afternoon, I returned to the hotel several hours before them. I unzipped my coat and sat on a couch facing an aquarium. For several minutes, I watched fish breach water's surface. One by one, they appeared to be coming up for oxygen, though I knew they were only filling themselves with air to keep buoyant. Otherwise, they would sink to tank's bottom, where there is no soil to bury them, making it always easier to flush them down the toilet.

Easier too now that my parents have both left me here, still wondering about men in delis, to fly back to Colorado and walk naked without them in the hot springs, to heal myself without them. All I have to do is buy myself a plane ticket in order to walk there again and feel my skin warmed by travertine, limestone long softened by heat and from which stalactites straggle. Unlike other forms of limestone, travertine never turns to marble. It sits too near the earth's entry to the underworld to grace any cathedral.

202

An hour before a man wearing a vest overhung with tassels drove us to take waters long infused with minerals, I changed into my Speedo in our hotel room's bathroom. There in my privacy, my vagina imprinted a milky mandorla onto my suit's fabric. I still emboss nearly every bathing suit or pair of panties with this same almond, which represents Christ's aureole in Christian iconography, my parents' religion. Most of us, though, recognize its shape as a vulva, its white seal that stains the cotton.

There where no one could see me, I bent down to smell the life of my small, white wholeness. My life and no one else's. Because when you do not glow with a mandorla yourself for anyone to notice, you can still take comfort in a smaller one leached from your uterus, in the fullness you have birthed by virtue of being a woman. This residue you leave everywhere of blanched almonds.

My mom could not have known all the bathers would be naked, all except for ourselves and another family with young children. The man in the fringed vest drove us up so high up a mountain that the city's lights dimmed into sparse, orange embers from a fire we had missed as we stood among it. Yet still we could make out the hang of nipples and skeins of pubic hair once our eyes adjusted to the darkness. Still we could see couples caressing each other's spinal columns, men massaging a breast with one hand while reaching the other down deeper into the water's blackness.

Eight years before this, when I was fourteen, an oncologist had excised my mom's left breast. She told me only the day before she drove herself for surgery to a hospital in Indianapolis. I asked her a few times in the years that followed if she needed to return for another examination. Each time I asked, she only shook her head, refusing to foresee any complications, refusing to prevent what now seems what had to happen. I say this only because I have been so much changed by her absence, because I no longer know who I'd be f she had not left me early. So I can only assume that as soon as her surgery was finished, the cancer lurking in her lymph nodes began its metastasis. I can only assume she lived a little more than a decade afterward suffering in silence as her body inflicted its own violence. On our last vacation, she was secretly hurting.

Our last two days in Colorado, she wore a red knit sweater I bought her that year for Christmas. Inside it, her one real breast hung limp while the cotton she filled her left bra cup with pointed higher up toward her chin. She in turn had knit me an afghan I now stow deep inside my closet. In time, I know its stitching will slacken. I know eventually it will begin unraveling into moss looking dyed violet. Still I hate for my husband to hurry its ruin by wrapping himself with it. He is tall, just taller than the blanket, and stretches it over toenails he grows long so they won't graft inside his skin, toenails that might rip apart its stitches. I try to say this kindly yet always end up screaming.

Only once did I confront my mom's missing breast, when she changed clothes with her bedroom door open to the hallway and I saw it reflected in a mirror in passing. It resembled an eye socket missing its pupil somehow still staring. A socket stricken with blindness and robbed of its pink iris.

According to his diaries, Percy Bysshe Shelley once dreamt he saw a pair of eyes blink inside his wife's nipples. The dream prompted a fit of screaming calmed later only with ether. I learned this in college from a professor I had long, languorous dreams of fucking. I learned this then made the mistake of sharing it with my mom one Thanksgiving as my dad carved the turkey. She soon left the dining room for the kitchen. When she returned, I could see she'd been crying.

Whether Shelley's death by sea before he turned thirty fulfilled a suicidal dream or was only deluded seafaring in the face of a storm clearly coming, his heart famously didn't burn on the funeral pyre his friends built off the coast of Italy. The rest of him charred like the offal of any other body, yet his heart resisted the flames. It avoided incineration but did not succeed at living.

For years his wife, Mary, kept what the fire could not consume wrapped in silk on her desk, while of my mom I have considerably less remaining. I hardly look as if I could be her daughter, people tell me. I have two breasts, but with neither can I see her clearly. The few pictures I have of her only remind me how ugly I'm growing in comparison. She was so lovely, so slender, even if her bottom half bulged as she grew older, growing as round as a water droplet falling down a mountain while one breast watched and the other saw nothing.

As my mom and I continued standing in the water, as close to the earth's inner fire as we would ever come together, I asked her where the steamboats had all gone, though we both knew there had never been any. I asked only to distract her from my dad looking toward other women with no eyes at their nipples to see him looking. I told myself this was the last time I would ever travel with my family.

After looking up at the stars to think about her answer, she turned toward me with her face lit into a laugh and said it was false advertising, wasn't it? In place of any steamboats, there were only bubbles in the water bursting from the earth's furnace. The steam smeared everything that once seemed solid into ghosts of memory too early in the making.

We're too old for this, my mom said when we walked inside our hotel lobby an hour later. I knew she meant only that she hadn't wanted to see all those slim, young bodies through steam continually shape-shifting, steam itself supple and copulating. If this was falling, it was not the kind of falling she wanted, into water heated so hot by rock that at first we'd hesitated to leave the ice where we stood barefoot.

In the 19th century, fur trappers straying into this corner of Colorado thought the steam arising from the hot springs came instead from steamboats coursing along a river as yet unseen, a river never since discovered. Even steam, however, cannot hover forever above trees that themselves grow only so tall before they collapse of their own height or simply tire of growing. And we all must fall eventually from the weight of our own fullness. Shattering is the price we all pay from approaching wholeness. Of all the lies we tell our ourselves, none is less honest than pretending nature doesn't like inflicting damage, that there are not predators haunting even bakery doorways, always among us.

Our last day, my parents both asked if I wanted to ski before we flew back that evening. They reminded me it might be my last chance for who knew how many years to come. Overspreading a bagel with cream cheese, I said I'd stay inside and read. I preferred the fireplace to the mountains for the time being, I added, as they refilled their coffee. I'd enjoy the lodge even more if I first went skiing, they suggested, so I told them that yesterday I'd seen blood dotting the slopes in splotches. They reminded me that we were eating, and I said no more about it.

The red snow, I know now, was only snow overlaid with a species of algae rich in carotenoids, the same as those found in carrots. As the algae grows and the snow's blush deepens, snow begins to smell as well as look splattered with watermelons. And in dreams I've had since my first menstruation, I am standing naked on a balcony ready to throw them. I am poised to toss a pile of watermelons onto a street as white as our last Colorado morning. Pedestrians are my only problem.

Dropping the fruit, I'm aware even in my sleep, may kill any number of innocent victims. Still the watermelons are growing on vines overspreading the carpet in the room behind me. They are threatening to push me off the balcony. Eventually I decide to throw them, risking fatalities as well as exposing myself to onlookers below. Yet as soon as the first watermelon is about to smash into a man reading a newspaper, he disappears and all of humanity with him. The streets and sidewalk are silenced in snowfall while I stand there and shiver, still hurtling watermelons that have begun wrapping their tendrils around the iron of the wrought iron balcony. I'm left with no choice except to keep turning the snow a deeper shade of scarlet.

And much as I'm wary of facile dream interpretations, it is red, all of it. Algae growing below snow and blood flowing monthly from my uterus, always red running beneath the surface—of skin and snow and water heated by rock itself burning deep within the planet. And in the white and blue of Colorado, I was starved for redness, for evidence of the earth's own inner throbbing. Rather than skiing, I wanted to sit in front of the fire all afternoon lost in sexual fantasies I could not indulge when traveling with my parents. I was captivated more by the fire than any mountains at breakfast.

That night, we flew back to Indianapolis through a light snowstorm. The defroster in the car we'd parked at the airport had stopped working, so I cleared the fog from the windshield with my hands as my mom drove us home. Just keeping wiping, she told me, when the highway began to recede then vanish. The hot springs' steam had followed us, she said, almost laughing. By the time we turned up our driveway, our breaths had hardened into something nearly solid, into crystals so clear at the windows' edges we saw nothing through them.

Acknowledgments

The Memory of Water first appeared as *Paddle Happy* in *Beetroot Journal.*

Courtesans in New Orleans first appeared as *Sleep's End* in *Barely South Review.*

Cave Dwellings first appeared in *Tin House Open Bar.*

April's Autumn first appeared as *Headlight Eyes* in *Headlands.*

The Etymology of Honey first appeared in *Riding Light Review.*

Weeping Virgin first appeared in *The James Franco Review.*

Pterodactyls at Flight first appeared as *Pterodactyls on Planes* in *Gone Lawn.*

Stray Tigers first appeared in *Flyover Country Review.*

Two Plastic Ponies first appeared in *Queen Mob's Tea House.*

Antlers in Space first appeared in *Souvenir Lit Journal.*

Underwater Bees first appeared in *pioneertown.*

Painted Metal Birds first appeared as *Whirl, Dervish, Whirl* in *Lowestoft Chronicle.*

Eel Electric first appeared as *Playing Astronaut* in *Atlas and Alice.*

A Silent Film first appeared in *Gravel.*

Airplanes over Disneyland first appeared in *PANK.*

The Salt Mines first appeared in *Pinball.*

Whip the Bones first appeared in *Squawk Back.*

Healing Waters first appeared in *Mud Season Review.*

About the Author

Melissa Wiley grew up on a small farm in Indiana. Her creative nonfiction has appeared in literary journals including *DIAGRAM*, *The Offing*, *Drunken Boat*, *PANK*, and *Queen Mob's Tea House*. She lives in Chicago with her husband.

NOW AVAILABLE FROM

Split Lip Press

I Once Met You But You Were Dead
by SJ Sindu

Plastic Vodka Bottle Sleepover
by Mila Jaroniec

Because I Wanted to Write You a Pop Song
by Kara Vernor

I Am the Oil of the Engine of the World
by Jared Yates Sexton

forget me/ hit me/ let me drink great quantities of clear, evil liquor
by Katie Schmid

For more info about the press and our titles, please visit:

WEBSITE: www.splitlippress.com
FACEBOOK: facebook.com/splitlippress
TWITTER: @splitlippress

213